LIVING THE DREAM

in the Algarve, Portugal

ALYSON SHELDRAKE

Tadornini Publishing

FREE PHOTO BOOK

To view a series of free photographs which accompany this book, please visit our Algarve Blog website:

www.algarveblog.net/the-book

Contents

1. I Could Live Here   1
2. Why Portugal?   7
3. Try Before you Buy   15
4. The House That Became a Home   21
5. Moving Abroad   29
6. Planning to Move and Making it Happen   35
7. Sailing Away   41
8. Settling In   47
9. Meeting the Locals   53
10. The Famous and not so Famous   59
11. Learning the Language   65
12. When Language Goes Wrong   71
13. Trying to be Legal   77
14. Driving on the Right Side of the Law   83
15. What's the Weather Like?   91
16. Random Acts of Portuguese Kindness   97
17. Going Back to the UK for a Holiday   103
18. Returning Home   109
19. The X-rated Expats   117
20. Food and Drink   125
21. Things That I Have Learnt   133
22. Art and Photography in the Algarve   141
23. Kat the Dog   151
24. Abandoned Animals   159
25. The Village That Came Back to Life   165
26. How Much Does it Cost to Live Here?   171
27. The Risk of Fire   177
28. Healthcare   183
29. Entertainment   191
30. Beaches to Explore   197
31. Wonderful Walks   205
32. Local History   213
33. Festivals and Fairs   221
34. Christmas in the Algarve   229
35. Permanent Residents   237

36. Selling and Buying Again   245
37. Moving   251

Postscript: Brexit   259
Further Reading   261
Contacts and Links   263
Acknowledgements   265
Free Photo Book   267
Living the Quieter Algarve Dream   269
About the Author   271
Your Review   273

I Could Live Here

There is something about continually getting up at 6.30 a.m. in the dark, in the middle of winter, to get ready for work, that can really get you down after a while. It wasn't the job itself that was the problem, as I had reached the top of the education tree that I had always dreamed of climbing up; in a rapid series of career jumps that had left me quite startled and amazed. But pinned on the wall beside my computer at work was a photograph of the view from our kitchen balcony window in the Algarve, and I looked at that photograph every day and dreamed.

The photograph had been there on the wall for almost three years looking down at me, quietly reminding me daily of something bright and fresh that felt like 'home' already. I knew how the mole felt in the Wind in the Willows when he smelt his home again after a time spent away exploring with Ratty; every time we went back to stay in our house in the Algarve I would have a feeling of almost deliriousness mixed with raw excitement.

I would often be caught at my desk staring into space recalling the exact moment when you step off the plane at Faro airport; and experience the heady scent of the land and the heat of the sun which hits you as soon as you walk down the steps of the plane. And our house in the Algarve already felt like we were coming 'home' each time we arrived there and put the key in the door.

As I sat there dreaming, I could almost feel my shoulders begin to sink back down to their rightful place, and the tension ease from my neck. I could feel the warmth of the sun on my smiling upturned face; only to be startled back to reality by my personal assistant asking me a sudden question across the office floor.

It is a sober warning that I give to you right at the start of this book though. If you don't want the torment of knowing that 'home' is somewhere other than where you are currently living and working – then don't put all your money into a property in a foreign country and then try to carry on working somewhere else with the dream of 'one day' moving there to live. It will torture you every single day that you are not there; and every trip and holiday you make back there will make it feel more and more like home; and make you increasingly reluctant to return to the 'real world' and your working life.

Initially this wasn't our intention when Dave, my husband, and I first met; we both had good jobs in the Police, but we both had a wanderlust that had never really been satisfied before, and we began to travel and explore the world at every opportunity that we had. Our motto for our holidays was simple: 'never go back to the same place twice' and we travelled to many exciting places that we had only ever read about or longed to visit.

Venice had always been my dream destination, and it certainly lived up to the brochures and guidebooks. The Caribbean and Hong Kong soon followed, and our honeymoon in Cape Town was nothing short of spectacular. South Africa was a beautiful, stunning country with a landscape and culture that truly amazed us.

The contrast between the local poverty and extreme wealth though that was displayed all around us in South Africa left us disturbed and dismayed. We are unfettered tourists when we travel, we hate to sit on a tour bus or go on packaged organised trips; preferring to travel on local transport or hire a car and explore with our cameras and our feet. If we can experience something 'real' from a place, which is often more about finding something small and local rather than visiting huge tourist monuments and attractions; then we are both happy.

It was there in Cape Town that we first thought about living somewhere other than the UK once Dave retired from the Police. He was always going to be the career 30-year officer that he had joined to be; I, on the other hand, knew that the Police was going to be too restrictive for me; and I left soon after our wedding, after thirteen years serving as an officer, to pursue a longed-for career in education.

I think I surprised even myself, however, with how quickly I managed to rise within the field of education, as within a very short space of time I found myself as a Director of Education for the Church of England, responsible for over 130 schools in Devon. It was a dream job, with an excellent salary for a girl who had come from an extremely poor part of Birmingham and a working-class background.

The job came with long hours, high responsibility and many challenges, all of which I relished.

I have always valued 'down-time' in my life as a balance though; and I quickly implemented a system that allowed both myself and all my staff team to be able to take time off in lieu of the extra hours we all worked. That meant working very long hours every week during term times; and then being able to take a decent break during the school holidays. Do not be fooled, not every job in the education sector comes with built-in school holidays.

We had holidayed several times to Spain, for many of the same reasons that so many people go there on holiday. It is relatively cheap and very easy to travel there, the sun is almost guaranteed to shine, and the food and culture (away from the English bars and restaurants) is sufficiently different for you to feel that you are 'abroad'. The beaches, towns and villages and local people all add to that feeling of being on holiday; and allow you to relax and recharge the internal batteries. Although perhaps our batteries were getting rather flatter than we had initially thought.

It was after one such trip to Spain, after a particularly busy time in our lives, that we met friends who kindly but rather brutally said to us,

"Look at you pair, you look so tired, never mind you are off on holiday soon, you'll be able to have a nice rest."

We must have been looking particularly bad, as we replied to them,

"We've just come back from Spain … but where have you two been, you look amazingly well?"

And they did indeed look extremely relaxed and happy, tanned and glowing.

"Oh, we've just come back from the Algarve in Portugal. We have friends that have a little fisherman's cottage out there and they let us stay there for £100 a week," came their reply.

A quick conversation ensued with our friends, who promised to let us know if their friends would also let us stay there for the same price. A week later and our flights to Faro airport were booked and we were clutching a key and a set of directions!

✿๛✧ଓ✿

It was going to be another one of our one-off 'don't go back to the same place twice' trips. Having covered quite a lot of Southern Spain over several holidays, we naively thought that the Algarve was merely an extension of Spain, and we saw it as just another place to go and explore, intending to try somewhere else next time.

And then in the hire car, with a scruffy set of directions in hand, we set off from Faro airport towards our destination. There was a moment which is still set firmly in my mind as one of those 'gasp' moments when we rounded a corner into Ferragudo which was to be our home for the following week; when the bay of this little traditional fishing village opened out in front of us, with its boats bobbing in the harbour; and the little whitewashed village with its church sat proudly at the top of the hill appeared ahead of us.

It was a good job there wasn't a car behind us as we slowed down, took in the stunning view in front of us, and rather inarticulately and ridiculously both said "Wow!" at the same time.

It still has that effect on me almost twenty years later; this pretty little village with its winding cobbled streets, the harbour full of fishing boats, the central square with its little cafés and restaurants, and the beautiful long stretch of beaches tucked around the corner from the lifeboat station.

Every time I drive or walk around that corner and it all comes into view, it still makes me say 'wow' inside, and gives me a sense of calm and peace that nowhere else has quite managed to achieve.

We were in truth hooked from that moment on. The initial belief that this was going to be 'just another holiday' quickly turned into a magical week of exploring and discovery, as every day gave us new things to enjoy and experience, and every red circle on the map that we drew only led us on to another ten places that we wanted to visit.

That was the start of our love affair with the Algarve. From our stance of 'never go back to the same place twice' we calculated that we returned to 'our' fisherman's cottage seven times in the subsequent two-and-a-half years. It became the only place that we wanted to visit, as we started doing repair jobs on the cottage for the owners when we visited, left small items behind in storage in the spare room, and travelled back there more often than the owners themselves who had become friends, and laughed every time that we rang them up to enquire if the cottage was being used at all that month!

Dave and I had been holidaying in our adopted cottage for several years when suddenly the defining day arrived when we sat in the sunshine in the square at Ferragudo, looked around and both voiced to each other at the same time,

"I could live here."

I think up until that point it had probably been just a silently voiced 'one day' distant dream for both of us, however once we had both said it out loud and agreed with each other; suddenly it became one of those 'well why not?' ideas. An idea that kept leaping up like a happy thought and swirling around our brains each time we visited.

For various reasons, financially we suddenly had money in the bank having sold our house in the UK, and we were renting as we did not want to settle permanently where we were currently based.

This was quite a fatal combination as we started wandering around Ferragudo looking in estate agent windows and searching online and realising that our money would stretch much further in Portugal.

Luckily for us, we both wanted the same dream. I cannot imagine how difficult it must be for one person in a relationship to want that kind of lifestyle change but find that their partner does not have the same longing. We sat in the sunshine in our local café, looked around us and both felt the same dream beginning to emerge. This could be our future home one day. It sounded so exciting, a little bit daunting, but certainly something that could actually happen.

We began to seriously research, plot, scheme and daydream our way to the moment when we could pick up the keys to our own ideal place in the sun.

Why Portugal?

W e warn people when they come to stay at our house now to beware the Portuguese warm sunny magic that bewitches you and attacks all your senses - you may never be the same again. That moment when you wander down into the village, sit and have a coffee and relax, as you watch the world go by with the warm sun on your face; or the first time that you glimpse the blue shimmering sea from the top of the steps that lead down to the beach – those are the moments that get your heart racing and your mind wandering into the 'what if we lived here?' thoughts that can change forever your perspective on life.

So what makes Portugal so special? Certainly the weather is a big factor, and long summer days of uninterrupted sunshine help enormously, although we know it is not all sun – boy, can it rain here too. And if we are honest, those long hot summers can even sometimes be too hot, as we sit in the shade with the locals and reminisce about the cooler autumn days, and long for the start of September.

The weather is gorgeous here all year round really with an average temperature well over 30 degrees in the summer, with over

300 reported days of sunshine a year. It is an easy place to market and promote when it comes to the sunshine factor.

But it is so much more than the sun and the weather, as anyone spending any length of time here discovers.

There is a sense that the seasons, the land and traditional farming methods, and the church calendar still give this country its rhythm and pattern. You are never far from open countryside here in the Algarve, and we often hear a cockerel crowing from a neighbour's garden (even if he does sound somewhat constipated which always makes us giggle!). People often say this is what England was like fifty years ago, and there is a sense of timelessness about this part of the world as soon as you step away from the beach-front tourist areas.

I have given a talk now for several years to a large contingent of mostly American and Canadian visitors who convene at an international 'Live and Invest Overseas' conference. They are visiting Portugal with the aim of purchasing a property either to rent or to live in. I share with them the key reasons why we have fallen in love with this beautiful country, and it is not a difficult speech to write.

We have some of the most beautiful beaches and you can choose from tourist-focused large resorts that cater for holidaymakers, or you can explore some of the more isolated and deserted coves and small beaches that dot the 100 miles of golden Algarve coastline. There are limestone caves and grottoes only reachable by boat, and sparkling waters and tiny inlets with fishermen stood precariously on the edge of the cliffs above fishing for their tea.

We have a beautiful nature reserve, the Ria Formosa lagoon, which is over 170 square kilometres in size and home to hundreds of different birds; and beautiful mountain and coastal path and walks to enjoy. The wildflowers in the spring, alongside the beautiful almond and orange blossom and jacaranda trees, can almost make you think you have landed in a tropical paradise.

The wildlife here is often delightful and unexpected. White Storks nest all over the Algarve, and the sight of them soaring above you, or landing down on their nest and tipping their head back to create their unusual and startling 'clack-clack' greeting is amazing. Finding a local nest with babies inside and watching them almost double in size every week until they are ready to take off for their maiden flight is a wonderful experience.

You can also take a boat trip out to watch dolphins off the coast here, although we have also been lucky enough to spot them frolicking out in the sea just off our local Praia Grande beach in the warm afternoon sunshine.

We have seen buzzards, chameleons, geckos, turtles, flamingos, red foxes, hares, otters, badgers, wild boar, hedgehogs, grey herons, and all manner of garden birds.

The Algarve is also a golfer's paradise boasting some of Europe's finest championship golf courses, all set in magnificent surroundings, and many courses have breath-taking views of the coastline. 1966 was not just the year that England won the World Cup in football, it was also the year that Henry Cotton laid out the first golf course at Penina. Now there are over 40 courses for golfers of all ranges and abilities to enjoy, and golf is firmly established here as both a professional sport and leisure activity.

There are spa resorts, luxury five-star hotels, villas and small fishing cottages to stay in. Every style of budget and requirement can be catered for here; and it is also a popular and romantic location for a wedding celebration too.

We have beautiful historical villages with traditional old white-washed cottages, winding cobbled streets, and an unhurried pace of life. Moorish influences prevail, from the chimney pots to the magnificent castles, churches and 9th century Roman remains which are scattered across the region.

There are glazed and painted tiles, the *azulejos*, which decorate the facades of old buildings in virtually every city and town. Visit any church, palace, or sometimes even just walk past an old house and you will see these distinctively patterned ceramic tiles. Traditional arts and crafts can still be found throughout this region and are worth exploring and collecting.

The Algarve has an abundance of quaint shops, stalls and marketplaces to buy locally produced goods, and there are purpose-built shopping centres with designer merchandise outlets and exclusive boutiques.

You can find peace and quiet, cafés and restaurants, fine dining, exclusive five-star venues and a busy nightlife economy; and tucked away hidden beaches - and nothing is too far away here.

For the family, there are theme parks, water parks, zoos, and a host of attractions and days out to enjoy. There is a good local cultural scene here and Lisbon is less than three hours away for major concerts and events. The town of Silves is transformed into a medieval extravaganza every summer for ten days, and events like this are fabulous for both tourists and locals alike.

※⁂※⁂※

It is not just the place though; it is also the local people. Throughout the region there are gentle, kind, welcoming Portuguese people, whose lives seem to march to a different pace of life; they make the time to sit in the sun; greet their friends, pass the time of day on a park bench or in a coffee shop; and they reflect an era long passed away in many other countries. They are polite, reserved, proud of their culture and heritage, and always willing to help you. A walk past a local restaurant recently resulted in the waiter drawing us in and insisting on giving us a drink on the house; we hadn't been there for some months and an hour later we were still catching up on the latest news with him.

The Portuguese are also an interesting dichotomy as they drive everywhere (often badly - indicators? Pah! Who needs them?) but in the evening they like to 'promenade' and we love the fact that people stop and say *bom dia* or *boa noite* to you - and they smile at you too. It takes some getting used to after the UK and the fact that people often actively avoid even looking at you, let alone speak to you.

There is a different, gentler pace of life here, with the passing of time measured by the local church bells that ring every hour, followed by another church in the distance which chimes away three minutes later. Nobody seems to mind.

There's also a general sense of being able to find joy in the moment despite the lack of overall wealth. We stumbled across the start of a local festival last week, with traditional singing and dancing - the Portuguese do enjoy dancing. They twirl and spin for hours, proud of their costumes and heritage, there is no drunkenness or fighting, just honest old-fashioned family entertainment.

You can almost be forgiven for feeling guilty out here sometimes, there really is no problem at all with savouring a small espresso coffee for half an hour sat outside a café, no-one is going to hurry you to pay, or tut at you for not ordering any food. Every town and village have public benches and seats in all the right places to enjoy the view or watch the world go by.

I love the timings of the occupants of these benches; the old men will sit together in the morning commenting on the world together as they sit in the sunshine, presumably whilst their wives are home sorting out the house and lunch. You may feel indignant for a moment, until you remember that come the afternoon, the same benches will be occupied by the women, all sat together chatting and sharing their latest news too. No-one seems rushed or bothered, it is perfectly accepted - and even expected - that they will just sit there and chat. Suddenly the frantic pace of life in the UK seems faintly ridiculous.

And when you are walking along a deserted beach in November watching the sunset, and feeling the sense of calm and peace that only the luxury of free time can give you, with the waves rhythmically and gently curling along the edge of the sand, and you are watching the little birds that dart in and out of the edge of the waves scurrying along ahead of you - then you know that you have made the right choice and you are exactly where you need to be.

One of the other nice things about living here in the Algarve is being able to sit outside in the sunshine and enjoy a leisurely meal in a pretty restaurant, savouring a variety of good quality, simple and tasty food.

Sardines are a staple menu in the summer months, and Portimão and its many fish restaurants are renowned for their sardines. 8.50 euros will get you six sardines, a side salad, boiled potatoes and a hunk of bread which is more than enough to keep the hunger at bay.

Portugal is not a very wealthy country, but the Portuguese do like to eat well. You'll witness this if you ever attend a birthday party or other special occasion, as a highly impressive cake is practically guaranteed, along with huge plates of sweet and savoury dishes, often prepared and planned days in advance by several generations of the family together.

There are lots of foods here that are produced locally and some that are only found when they are in season - and they are worth waiting for. Figs, almonds, citrus fruits, sweet potatoes, local cheeses and breads, cured hams, olive oil and black pork, fresh fish, and olives, and not forgetting their famous port, and the delightful vinho verde and other locally produced wines.

Live and Invest Overseas has rated Portugal as the best place in the world to retire for four consecutive years. They state that the 'fantastic climate, great quality of life and low cost of living' are just some of the reasons why so many people choose to retire in Portugal.[1]

The Annual Global Retirement Index from International Living voted Portugal as the best place to retire in 2020 thanks to its low cost of living, climate and healthcare system. They highlight destinations from around the globe where you can 'live a healthier and happier life, spend a lot less money, and get a whole lot more'.[2]

Portugal is also rated as the third safest country in the world on the 2019 Global Peace Index, which makes the country not only a beautiful place to live but also a safe one too.

Not bad results for a little country that only has a total population of just over 10 million people, and a total figure of around 900,000 expats.

We're not completely smitten past the point of reality though - we know that the pace and the endless bureaucracy can get to you - especially after being used to the UK and different ways of doing things - and the language barrier continues to make everything more difficult (more about that in later chapters) ... but I hope that we are always able to 'enjoy the moment' here, to slow down and accept a different pace and way of doing things, and never forget why we fell in love with this special little place.

1. Live and Invest Overseas (s.d.). Website article *The Algarve, Portugal*. Accessed 1st February 2020 through https://www.liveandinvestoverseas.com/country-hub/portugal/the-algarve-portugal-retirement/
2. Cited via the Portugal News (10.01.2020). Website article by Daisy Sampson *Portugal Top for Retirees*. Accessed 1st February 2020 through https://www.theportugalnews.com/news/portugal-top-for-retirees/52603

3

Try Before you Buy

I always recommend that people move over here and rent for at least six months before they even think about buying a property or plan a permanent move. Renting, especially outside of the holiday season, will give you a much better feel for what living abroad would be like. It is so very different from being on holiday, and the weather and climate, paperwork, pace of life and traditions are very different from what you might be used to, and it can be quite a culture shock to suddenly finding yourself living in a different country.

Renting also gives you one enormous positive too – you can really find out what a place is like without making a huge financial or life-changing commitment. The lively town with bars and cafés open until 4 a.m. might be fine if you are on holiday, but if you find yourself awake half the night, or unable to sleep with your windows open at night in the middle of summer in the stifling heat because of the noise from a nearby late-night beach restaurant; you might decide that living somewhere quieter might actually be better!

Alternatively, you might have hankered for that quiet village house, dreaming of a life of peace and tranquillity, and then find that it is all a bit too quiet for you – especially in the winter.

We always recommend that you do your homework and find out

what somewhere is really like by renting before you buy. That way you will hopefully prevent any nasty shocks later. Although whilst I am writing these sage words of wisdom, I am smiling to myself as I try to put together the words 'renting' and 'nasty shocks' in the same sentence without laughing. Yes, you've probably guessed it, we failed to do our homework and had quite a surprise some years ago.

The little cottage we always rented was up for sale at one point, and we were rather concerned that we might not be able to stay there for our next planned holiday. As we had always stayed there, we had no other options stored away, and we wandered around the village late one afternoon wondering what we could do.

"I know, what about that *quinta* (farm) which is always advertising Bed and Breakfast at the edge of the village ... why don't we try there?" one of us brightly suggested.

So off we went and found the property which had a rather elaborate and impressive looking rope bell pull beside a large and rather formidable statue of a horse's head. A few good tugs on the rope and a loud tinkling sound could be heard from inside the grounds. We waited – and waited – and had almost completely given up and started walking away, when the wooden gates opened, and there stood a woman, leaning against the gate post, wearing an almost see-through kaftan.

"Yes, can I help you?" she said.

We both stood looking stupid, wondering how we could get out of this one promptly, when Dave said,

"Oh, we were just looking for some accommodation for a future holiday, but it's no problem, we can come back later."

"Oh no, that's alright, do come in," she said, "and have a look around now."

She waved her arm in the vague direction of the drive leading into the grounds of the property, inviting us to enter.

It is at moments like this that you suddenly find that your brain is saying 'leave ... now' and yet your legs start walking forwards ... and before you know it, you are inside the drive and the gates are shutting behind you, and kaftan-lady is wafting up the drive telling you all about the *quinta* and how many bedrooms it has, how many have en-suite bathrooms and how big the shared pool is. Followed by the classic line,

"We're all nudists here, that's not a problem is it?"

"Oh no, that's fine," I replied.

I mentally kicked myself, did I just really say that??!

You don't want to be rude, and kaftan-lady is being perfectly friendly and nice … but well, 'no actually, each to their own and all that, but no – not really – not for me' were the thoughts whirling around my head. We walk over to the gardens and pool area and are greeted by at least nine or ten naked people, who are all wandering around or sunbathing … and worse – firing up the barbecue … all with their various bits and pieces wobbling around.

I think it might actually have gone down as a record for them; how quickly one couple can look round an entire *quinta* full of bedrooms and gardens, march themselves back down the drive, thank kaftan-lady warmly whilst shaking her hand and then extricate themselves back out of the entrance gates without actually running. Or laughing. Loudly.

Next time we will check somewhere on the internet, or at least ask around, before we go visiting!!

And no – before you ask – we didn't go back there to stay!

✧ﾛ✧લ✧

As I have already described, dreaming of a life in the sun (whilst wearing at least a swimming costume!) and looking longingly into estate agent windows, quickly turned into house-hunting for us, and this is where we learnt about one of the uglier sides of buying abroad. I'm just glad we both have the police officer 'sniff them out' noses that give you that instinctive 'uh-oh' warning feeling about someone that so often proves itself to be true.

We had found a fabulous 3-bedroom penthouse apartment in a great block, only a five-minute walk from both the local beach and the village centre in Ferragudo. An apartment wasn't our first choice, and we had viewed several properties, but this was the first one that made us go back for a second and then a third look ... and it was advertised at a good price too.

We wandered round the apartment on our third viewing, deciding where we would place all our furniture, and had already mentally moved in. We sat down in the office with the sales assistant and bartered down the price to an even better deal, as she dealt with the builder on the other end of the phone. Then she said that the builder wanted to meet us to shake hands on the price and talk about the deposit and that he would be there in the office in ten minutes.

The moment he walked in, we both thought 'oh dear' and that was when everything went downhill fast. He told us that he would agree to our price if we put 40,000 euros of the total sale amount in cash in an envelope for him when we completed the sale. He made it sound like he was doing us a favour, and it was obvious that it would be beneficial to him, as presumably he would not be declaring that amount for tax purposes.

What we didn't realise at the time was how bad that would be for us down the line when we tried to sell the apartment again, as the purchase price would obviously show 40,000 euros below the total we had paid. Should we sell at a break-even price to us, if we decided to then take the money out of Portugal, we would have to pay capital gains tax on all the profit. In effect that undeclared 40,000 euros would have come back to bite us at that point, as that would have shown as an 'extra' amount that we would have had to pay tax on as 'profit'.

We did not know any of this at the time; we just had an instinct that kicked in that said, 'no thank you'. That's not how we like to do business, as anyone that knows us will tell you; we have always tried to do things properly – and legally. When we said 'no thanks' to the 40,000 euros in the envelope and his very kind offer; the builder instantly turned nasty and started threatening to put the price up.

We calmly, but sadly, told him we were no longer interested, and walked away. It was a beautiful apartment, and we drive past it most days, and sometimes look up and wonder 'what if?' But we were happy that we had been true to ourselves and our instincts, and later once we realised what the tax implications would have meant, we were even more comfortable with our decision to walk away.

It was however an exhausting experience emotionally, as it is surprising how quickly a property that you are 'just looking at' can become 'home' in your mind, even before you have signed anything on paper. However, that wait proved to be so beneficial to us, as we found the much larger, spacious, bright house full of light and space and potential, which became our home instead. It is funny how things work out in the end.

That house is now home for my art studio, the dream I have always had of having my own creative studio space has finally come true; and Dave has a fantastic photographic studio space and we share a large office space. All that; and four bedrooms, a massive outside space and a stupendous view; surrounded by lovely Portuguese neighbours.

It is quite a strange feeling buying a house abroad, somehow it doesn't seem quite as real as buying in the UK, and it is something that we know some people can only dream about doing. The other side of this is that sometimes you must be brave, and a bit foolhardy, and a little bit crazy to do something different – but the rewards are there if you are willing to go for it. For us, we knew that financially, and work wise, we couldn't just up sticks and run away to live there straight away, we still had jobs and commitments and lives in the UK, but it became our passion and desire, that 'one day' we would move to the Algarve, to live in our house and start living our dream.

It was just going to take time to achieve this and for us to be in the financial position to be able to do it. It took a further five years before we made the permanent move here. But it gave us a great incentive to work towards and it also gave me that fabulous photo to pin to the wall of the office at work to keep me focused and drive me crazy until we could finally move here to live.

4

The House That Became a Home

We hadn't specifically planned to buy a house when we came out here one August summer holiday for our annual dose of summer sunshine. We had been so busy with work we decided that we wouldn't house-hunt at all, we would just have a break in the sun. Added to that the disappointment we still felt every time we walked past the apartment we had nearly bought - and which was still for sale - meant that we were happy to put our house buying plans on hold for a few months.

So there we were, sat in the square on our first day out here relaxing, when an estate agent we knew came bounding up to us and said,

"I've got just the house for you."

"Oh no," we told her, "we're just out here for a break."

But she insisted, and we agreed to see it, more to keep her happy to be honest than with any great desire to see anything for sale.

She arranged to meet us that afternoon and gave us directions. The property was on the edge of the village, in a small urban area that was not over-developed, and which we had never really explored as it was not one of the main routes for us as we travelled around. She told us that the owners were Portuguese and keen to sell. We met her at the property and looked around with interest. The area was residential, established and quiet. It did not have the look or feel of a holiday zone, and it was ticking all our external requirement boxes nicely. The house seemed to be a large property, and modern. We were keen to look inside.

The estate agent was very clever though as she opened the front door and led us straight upstairs to the back balcony, which had the most stunning views across to the nearby town of Portimão and all the way to the distant hills and town of Monchique. It was a clear sunny day and it was truly breath-taking how far we could see. We toured the bedrooms and the main ground floor, and it had everything we wanted; and as we turned to leave the estate agent said,

"But you haven't seen it all yet, follow me."

She took us downstairs to what the Portuguese call the 'cave' or indoor garage – and which we would call a separate two-bedroom apartment! Another surprise, and one which had potential written all over it. All that; and four bedrooms, a massive outside space and a stupendous view; surrounded by lovely Portuguese neighbours.

We stood in the garden area, which was nothing more than an overgrown wilderness, with waist-high weeds, and tried to imagine what it would look like with a little work done on it. The house from the front looked big enough, it was two stories and semi-detached, with a nice small front garden area. But from the back you could see the actual size of the whole property as it stretched up three stories high at the rear. The main garden area was about 50 metres wide by 100 metres long, which included a steep drive down to the garage door.

It was an amazing property; and the price was not much more expensive than the price of the apartment we had rejected. We told the estate agent we would let her know.

We drove back again that evening and sat opposite the house in our hire car listening and looking. A couple of neighbours waved to us, everything was peaceful, the view was even more stunning at night, looking across at the twinkling lights of Portimão, and the house looked perfect.

We did the maths, chewed it over and made a daft offer which was accepted.

We knew that the paperwork would take some time and our deadline for returning to the UK to return to work was fast approaching. We asked around and a solicitor in a nearby town was recommended to us, so we went off to meet someone who turned out to be a real character, but who served us well.

She was Brazilian, in her 50's and chain-smoked for the entire meeting. She had paper and folders piled up all around her small office, had a rasping smoky deep voice and lots of attitude. She talked no nonsense, explained everything simply, and we liked her enough to hire her there and then to sort out the purchase of the house for us.

We met her at a local notary office the next day, which was our first experience of Portuguese bureaucracy and their love of paperwork. We insisted that we wanted to jointly purchase the house, which is not that usual in Portugal, but as we are a couple who always share everything financially, that is the way we wanted to do it. We gave the solicitor power of attorney, paid her a deposit, signed a small rain forest in paperwork, and suddenly we were on the plane back to the UK and our dream of buying a house was suddenly about to happen.

September and October passed by quickly, however we discovered that buying a house in Portugal can take a lot longer than that. We were arranging a mortgage which should have been a simple process, using a bank that had offices in both London and Lisbon. After weeks of waiting and not hearing anything, we contacted them to find out what was wrong.

We found out that the Portuguese bank had no idea what a Premium Bond was, which was where we had profitably stashed our cash after selling our home in the UK. A bond in Portugal is something that ties up your money for at least five years; and cannot be accessed in the meantime. We had explained to the bank that the company in charge of Premium Bonds would release the money we had invested within five to seven days if required, but this explanation had not satisfied them, so they had shelved our application. Without asking us. We had to ask the Premium Bonds company themselves to write a letter to the bank confirming that they could release funds quickly when requested. The bank finally agreed to our mortgage request and we could move forward.

A strong British pound to euro conversion rate was in our favour at the time, and our solicitor asked us to transfer over 80,000 euros to her bank account so that she could complete the sale. I happily wired over the money without a thought, until Dave commented,

"She's probably booking her ticket to Rio de Janeiro as we speak. We might never see her or our money again!"

Eek! Thanks Dave. How to make a girl in charge of the household finances panic. And then finally the mortgage paperwork was through, our solicitor was happy, everything had been paid and was confirmed – and on Dave's 50th birthday – it was ours! We had done it; we had bought a house in Portugal.

○ ʂ ○ ʗ ○

We travelled out as soon as we could to pick up the keys and explore our new home. Walking into an empty house with no furniture was eerie. Sounds echoed and the space seemed enormous to fill. We rented an apartment nearby on that trip until we could travel out again and spend time furnishing and decorating, as we literally had no furniture at all.

If 'home is where the heart is' then our home most definitely became in Portugal from that moment. Buying was a relatively simple process, but then locking up and driving away back to the airport after that first trip out to pick up the keys most definitely wasn't easy. It became harder and harder to leave each time we visited, especially once we had bought furniture and made the house more homely; and started leaving clothes and belongings behind each time we left.

One of our defining moments was the time we travelled out to Portugal for three weeks for a summer holiday break. We had a relaxing wonderful time, and we were sad to lock up and leave our home to travel back to the airport. When we arrived there, we sat in the departure lounge waiting for our flight to be called. We were renowned for taking the very last flight possible back to the UK at the end of each break. If we had to be back at work on a Monday morning, we would book the 7.30 p.m. flight back for the Sunday evening. We waited and waited, but no announcement was made, and then an attendant walked around and told everyone waiting for the flight,

"We are sorry to report that the co-pilot was taken ill on the flight, he has been rushed to hospital, and we cannot find a replacement to accompany the pilot back home this evening. We are sorry but you will have to return tomorrow morning for your flight. We can arrange accommodation for you if required."

Oh, accommodation not required thank you! We called our hire car company, I explained the situation, and we were in luck as we discovered that the rental car was still where we had left it in the drop-off section of the car park. The rental company agent agreed to meet us back there and half an hour later we had the car keys back in our hands. We gleefully danced a jig around the car, then collapsed laughing when we realised that we were getting excited about staying for one more night back in our house, after three long weeks there. We drove all the way back, camped out, and drove back the next morning to the airport to board our flight.

We decided that we had better start planning to move out to Portugal to live permanently as we had always intended to, or perhaps go nuts in the process of waiting.

✿ɷ✦ଔ✿

The contrast between life in the UK and 'home' in Portugal became starker after this episode.

'Home' was where we could wander the cobbled streets, being greeted warmly by the locals, and where elderly people sat on benches in the sun, smiled and said *bom dia* to you as you walked by. Suddenly the frantic bumping and jostling of people passing you on the street in the UK was too much to bear.

'Home' was where the still warm *pastel de nata* pastry was

accompanied by a tiny espresso and an hour (or two!) of sitting outside a local café watching the world pass by. Suddenly the bucket sized coffee from the super-size-me coffee shop on the High Street seemed faintly ridiculous.

'Home' was where shopping for dinner involved wandering around the local market, picking up local produce in season and selecting amazing fresh fish almost straight from the boat at such a low price. Suddenly the pre-packaged food and ready meals from the giant UK supermarket looked and tasted like plastic.

'Home' was where you could sit outside in the sunshine and enjoy a leisurely lunch with friends with a chilled glass of wine, and where the heady scent of blossom filled the air. Lunch at work usually involved eating a soggy sandwich at about 3.30 p.m. before dashing out the door to the next meeting.

'Home' was where our exercise consisted of long walks on the beach, walking barefoot along the edge of the sand where the waves gently curled onto the shore, feeling the warm sun on your face. Or even sometimes a full pelt, dive in quick then enjoy a gentle swim in the almost cold sea water, surrounded by a shoal of tiny darting silver fish. Time and the inclination to exercise in the UK was always non-existent.

And 'home' was where our neighbours gave us bags of fresh lemons and oranges, figs and home-made cake, helped us to dig over our garden and gave us plants and compost. Our neighbour in the UK smoked dope and played loud music and computer games all night.

Small wonder then that the call of our 'home' in Portugal became louder and more insistent!

And 'home' held another dream too, one that burned away inside me. Our house had space for the art studio I had always wanted, together with the most precious thing of all – time. Time to relax; time to paint; time to enjoy life – and time to simply 'be'.

It was a simple choice after all, not a 'lucky' choice or a 'brave' choice and we are definitely poorer now if you define that simply as how much money you have in your bank account, but we are rich beyond measure in comparison to our old life in the UK.

But if we are asked 'Why have you moved abroad?' we have a pretty simple answer that we can give now. We have fallen in love with a beautiful country and people; and we wanted to experience a simpler, slower, richer, and more gentle way of life. Who knows how it will all turn out in the end? But at least we will never have those haunting 'what if?' or 'I wish we had' thoughts in the future.

So the only advice that I can really give you is this: if your heart is buried in the sand on a distant beach – if you have a picture of 'your beach' on your computer at work – and you can hear the pull of a distant shore gently but insistently calling you 'home' – and if your friends say to you "You must be mad" – then it is probably time to start packing!

5

Moving Abroad

The dream of living abroad for many people remains just that - a dream. We were determined to do something brave and bold and different, so that we wouldn't look back with a sense of regret later in life. Once we had made the decision to buy a property abroad, with the plan to move there in the future, things seemed to fall into place quite easily. This helped us with the overall feeling that we were doing the right thing, although the number of people who said to us "Oh you're so brave, I couldn't do that", made us feel for a while that we really were doing something rather foolhardy or epic - rather than actually just planning to live somewhere else in Europe.

There is a strong piece of advice that we give to everyone though before they even think about moving to live abroad. Do your homework, research, ask questions, ask local people and other 'expats', look online, ask more questions, do more research – and critically for us – have a plan of what you want to do when you get there.

We instinctively seemed to know that living abroad is so different from going on holiday, and we also knew from the start that we wanted to 'do something' when we arrived in Portugal. We were both too young to just 'retire' although technically that was what

Dave would be doing when he finished his police career. He was often being teased by me about 'becoming a pensioner' in his early fifties. My thought process was a simple one, namely that when he had a pension, he would, by definition, therefore, be a pensioner. I have often threatened to buy him one of the flat fisherman's hats that all retired men in Ferragudo village seem to wear as a badge of honour once they have retired from work.

We didn't want to move abroad and be bored. There are only so many cafés and restaurants you can visit, or even afford to visit, and neither of us enjoy just sunbathing. We don't play golf, certainly couldn't afford a lavish lifestyle, and we have both always been very active and busy people. Too busy probably, and we certainly didn't want to be working that hard again. But having every day stretch out in front of us with a blank diary also didn't seem like a plan for us.

Luckily, we both had long-held dreams of transforming our hobbies into something more concrete and professional once we moved out here to live permanently. We had no idea if our plans would be successful, but at the very worst, they would keep us busy and out of mischief, and give our days some purpose and opportunity.

Our dreams of starting our own art and photography business were tempered with a financial reality check, however. We were under no illusion of the finances that would be required to be able to live a comfortable life out here, and of how difficult it would be to run any sort of business in a foreign country where you can barely speak the language, where the average monthly wage is around 650 euros a month, and where most of the local jobs are at best seasonal and transitory.

We tried to plan and budget as much as we could before we made the leap and tried to factor in the unpredictable nature of the British pound to euro exchange rate as well. Dave's pension would be taxed at source as a Local Government Pension, we had no wriggle room with this as that is just how the pension is organised. It would mean that the exchange rate each month on 'pay day' would be critical to us. We planned our finances around what we thought would be the worst-case scenario - that being a one-to-one pound-to-euro exchange rate. Little did we realise how important that frugal planning would become in the future, as the idea of Britain leaving Europe was not even a remote possibility when we purchased our house back in 2006.

The other side of the Euro coin though was some great advice given to us by someone who had already made the move to live out here. It was plain advice, but it struck a chord with us and it was this simple sentence which they said to us,

"If you wait until you can afford to live out here, you will never make the move."

In other words, you can do all of the financial planning and research, saving and financial forecasting, and organising that you want to, but there will always be a 'if we can just save up for that, or just wait for that bond to mature, or wait for that deal to go through' mentality … and eventually you will look back many years later and realise that you are still stuck in the same place, and your dream of living abroad is still that – just a dream. We were very determined to make our dream a reality, with all the financial implications, planning and saving that entailed, and then finally just taking a deep breath and going for it.

✧๛✧ଓ✧

Several things happened around us at that time that made us determined to buy our dream property and move abroad. Going to the funeral of a colleague aged only 41, who had died of cancer leaving a wife and young family behind; was a heart-breaking and seminal moment for both of us. Realising that life goes by in a flash, that it can be taken away so suddenly and cruelly, and that, as far as we know, you only get one crack at life here; together with experiencing a sudden and unexpected loss like that, really makes you question what life is really all about.

There is an interesting idea that I found online of a writer who added a 'life countdown' to his computer screen homepage, which advised him that he had 8,500 days left to live and counting[1]. As none of us can know how much time we have left on earth (he gambled on living to age 78) it is a difficult calculation to make; however the idea of living in the present and enjoying what we have now, is certainly not a bad life motto to follow.

We bought a painted sign long before we left the UK which now takes pride of place on our office wall, and which says 'Some people want it to happen, some people wish it would happen, some people make it happen' and it is a real affirmation for us that we would be doing the right thing in moving out here to live.

There is a lovely simple phrase which implores you not to 'miss out on yourself' and there's something wonderful in that exhortation; with its reminder that we each have gifts and talents we need to make sure we have used up, wrung out and hung out to dry before our lives are over. Our lives were so busy that the hobbies that we loved were side-lined for years. I have always loved to paint, managing to fit in the occasional art class or course; gaining my love back again and being inspired, only to pack all the paints back away again once it is time to go back to work. Dave held a similar dream to be able to spend time with his camera, enjoying his love of photography, and seeing where his talents might take him.

We had also both been inspired by a movement online to encourage a more minimal lifestyle. The idea of living a simpler, less complex and less stressful way of life was most appealing. Perhaps it was the years and years of shift-work; the sights and situations only someone in the Emergency Services ever gets to experience and has to deal with, the long hours, constant pressure and critical decision-making that come with responsible jobs, and posh-sounding job titles that can take a toll on even the most sane and balanced person.

Added to that, the feeling of being a hamster in a wheel, buying the requisite house, the car and the possessions 'necessary' to balance the job and life you have created, and then realising that you are trapped in that job until you have paid off everything that you have bought; only to then buy more and start the wheel turning all over again, can leave you feeling drained and exhausted.

What I have discovered along this journey though is that you do not even realise that you are the hamster, or that you are in that cage, until you step back, move outside of that life, and stand away from the edge long enough to look back at that time in your life with the hindsight of a period of reflection; and it is only then that you can see the poor hamster in its wheel spinning rapidly round and realise 'that was me'.

Sadly what you then start to see is that so many of your friends are also stuck in the same cage, going around and round the same wheel. This change of lifestyle is not easy though, and I wouldn't want people to read this, and march into work the next day and hand in their notice. We spent several years planning, talking, saving, making other sacrifices, and working hard to convince family and friends that this is really what we wanted to do.

It can also come across as a selfish decision and can require some tempering and careful decision-making along the way. Suffice to say that we sadly lost some friends on the journey, who for whatever their reasons; just didn't keep in touch with us or want to be part of the cheering crowd at the departure gate. Other friends I am sure were glad to see the back of us!

---

1. Kevin Kelly (s.d.). Website article *My Life Countdown*. Accessed 15th March 2020 through https://kk.org/ct2/my-life-countdown-1/

6

Planning to Move and Making it Happen

The last month in our flat in Devon found me weeping with laughter when I really should have been crying with frustration. It was also the moment when Dave realised why absolutely all of the accounts and service providers at our flat were originally signed up in either my name, or our joint names, except one which was solely in his name ... that would be our Sky TV subscription. This ensured that every time we had to call them, Dave had to be the brave person dragged to the phone and left to call their 'Customer Service helpline'. I do think the Trades Description Act should be enforced here ... it's a bit like Inspector Fowler on the Thin Blue Line television series calling his 'credit card instant speedy hotline' ... and shouting at them that they were neither 'instant nor speedy'. And Sky TV, in our experience, are most certainly not helpful nor do they seem to serve the customer well. I don't think they serve you at all if you are trying to cancel something; they seem fine if you are trying to buy something.

After 85 minutes (at 5p per minute) talking to a young lad who had been specially trained in the art of fobbing Dave off, and who was refusing to transfer him through to a supervisor, and also refusing point blank to cancel our Broadband, we gave up with that approach and tried the email attack. The fact that we were literally leaving the country to a destination that did not even have Sky TV as an option, seemed irrelevant to their helpline. We were fully paid up, did not have a contract that had any time left to run, and still they did not want to cancel our account. We had contacted the bank in desperation and cancelled the direct debit, so they would not have any more money from us - but still - we just wanted our account cancelled!

The next step would have been to email Rupert Murdoch direct on his ocean-cruising yacht and resorting to just posting the television box and cards back to Sky. We even looked up the postal address and worked out how much that would cost to do. If you want to send a chill down your spine if you are a Sky customer, just Google 'cancelling sky subscription' and read some forums.

Eventually, after many painful days of phone calls and emails, we did eventually manage to cancel the account ... or so we thought. After about two years of living here, we happened to click on an old email programme and realised that for the previous two years, Sky had been faithfully downloading and helpfully saving all - and I mean all - of our emails to our 'old' Sky email account. Turns out that the helpful souls at Sky are concerned that you might not have actually really definitely wanted to cancel your email account, even though you have quite clearly told them that ... yes you definitely do want to cancel, no you don't want to have 30 days to decide, and no you definitely won't be coming back to them, because they don't actually have coverage in the Algarve in Portugal. We whizzed down through the first 4 or 5,000 emails and gave up. Probably somewhere, in a parallel email galaxy rolling along beside us, we are still getting Sky emails delivered.

Other companies on the 'to cancel' list were far more helpful and we slowly managed to wade through it all. It is amazing just how much there is to sort out and every day we thought of another thing to do. It involved writing lists and more 'to do' lists, and even eventually a more urgent 'what we haven't done' list. I cannot underestimate just how long it takes to cancel your online, virtual and financial life in one country before moving abroad.

We also sold lots of furniture on eBay, which was really good fun. It did mean a frantic emptying of a piece of furniture before the buyer could collect it (the wardrobes were fun!) and then packing everything into even more boxes. Our flat looked like it had been burgled and I gave up hope of finding anything I needed about four weeks before our actual removal day.

But suddenly we only had 4 more weeks to go to the big removal date. Which equated to 28 more sleeps; 11 more working days for me; 1 more haircut; and 6 leaving parties at work to survive in one week. And lots of final meals out with friends which was lovely. We joked that we would have to start a serious diet once we arrived in Portugal, just to counteract all of the fabulous meals out we had before we left, although I managed to make sure that I could fit in just a few more Bakewell Tart cakes from our favourite café in Honiton before we left. There were not many foods that I knew I was going to miss but their cakes were definitely on the list.

Then came a significant and slightly scary moment when we arrived home from work one afternoon and I realised that in only one week's time I would be 'unemployed'; that in two weeks' time we would be 'homeless'; and in under three weeks' time we would be living in Portugal! I think it was made all the more poignant by the fact that our flat was full of boxes and bare walls (very strange for two people who love art) and we realised that it really was happening and we were about to move abroad to live - full time.

✿ཽ✿ଔ✿

The last few weeks before we moved were an interesting mix of emotions and goodbyes, however every few days something else annoyed me and reminded me why we had made the decision to move abroad. The list became a long one:

Driving in the UK - we were almost wiped out on the motorway by a crazy driver pulling out in front of us. The best bit was that she veered out, saw us late in her mirror, veered back into the middle lane, then ... pulled out in front of us anyway! Oh, and no apology of course. What I find interesting is that we experience driving just like that in Portugal and it doesn't bother us in the same way at all.

Shopping in the UK - why is everyone is such a hurry?! And why does the UK service sector so often consist of people employed who look like the last thing they want to do is help you or serve you?

Cafés in the UK - why do they all shut at 4.30 p.m.?! That's just the time I always want to go and unwind with a coffee and a slice of cake and all you can see are tables and chairs stacked up ready for the café to shut. Imagine that in Portugal - unthinkable! Most cafés here open at 7 a.m. and are still going strong at 10 p.m.

The great British public when the sun comes out is another strange absurdity and the sights in the summer months can be quite something. Why do men always think it's fine to take their top off as soon as the sun comes out and why is it always the men who shouldn't take their top off that are first up? (It's enough to put me off that slice of cake in the late afternoon ... if only I could buy one!)

TV advertising - I will be happy if I never hear another 'go compare'; or see another inane grinning bloke dressed up as a very dodgy ballroom dancer with the strangest accent ever; or see another 'have you had an accident, did you trip over the giant mop and bucket right in front of your nose?' - don't worry 'sue everyone' advert. Although I know that the Portuguese indulge in 20 minute advert breaks on their television channels; but they do actually warn you that they are about to start and often helpfully tell you how long the ad break is going to last - and it is nice to see that their TV adverts are as bad as ours!

❀ɷ❀ଓ❀

Suddenly there was only one week to go before our moving day. For me it had been the week that had been circled in the diary for so long ... and then oh so quickly it was all over. Leaving day, or rather 'leaving week' as it turned out to be, was a chance to reflect on my work and spend time with lovely people, and then quietly leave (well maybe not so quietly as my team would have told you). But actually saying goodbye seemed a strange idea as so many people I had worked with had become friends and; along with many dear friends that we had known for so long already; we always intended to keep in touch with them all through Facebook, Skype and email. The internet seems to make people so much closer and easier to reach, I'm sure even ten years ago leaving for a different country would have felt so much more final and isolating ... instead we just felt like we were moving to a new house.

I also treated myself to a Kindle as I am an avid reader. It is a great little piece of kit (and I am such a gadget girl, so it made me very happy!) and the books descend in seconds. It is hard to find lots of English books abroad so it was important to me to know that I could still read lots of books once we landed in Portugal. It was also an interesting experiment in deciding which books I was happy to download as oppose to which I could not physically live without and wanted to pack and ship over with us. Lots of children's classics (all free!) including Black Beauty, Alice in Wonderland, the Jungle Book, and Pinocchio were downloaded alongside The Complete Sherlock Holmes; and Walt Whitman's poems. It's amazing how much of my childhood is evoked through these books.

ೋౡ෴೦ಞ෴

The last few days in the UK were challenging, exhausting and exciting, and usually all three emotions combined at the same time. I thought it might be useful for anyone else contemplating the same journey to have a few hints and tips to enjoy along the way - these are all things we found useful to know - or in most cases things we wish we had known about in advance so that we could avoid them or do things differently:

Handing in your notice from your job is the easy bit – the hard bit is deciding to do it.

Once you have told people you are leaving at work – things change – and you change. It's inevitable. There's a 'peeling away' that happens emotionally and sometimes physically. That's ok; it helps you all move on.

However much you plan and research you can never fully sort out all your finances and budget until you have moved.

You can never have too many cardboard boxes when you are packing, beg and borrow them from anywhere. And the free newspapers you find outside the supermarkets are perfect for scrunching and packing boxes with. It's worth ordering a mountainous supply of big bubble wrap and builders' gaffer tape.

It will take you six times as long to pack a room up as you think, mainly due to the 'oh I wondered where that had gone' moments which seem to coincide conveniently with tea and biscuit breaks!

You will end up with at least six times as many boxes as you thought you would have.

The removal company in our case consisted of a very happy couple of chaps and a huge van with a trailer and still we managed to have more stuff packed than space to pack it into. We ended up having to find some willing friends to babysit two pedal cycles for us until the next time the van company happened to be travelling to Portugal.

There will probably be something that doesn't fit into the removal van that you decide that you don't really need and leave behind – and it will definitely be something that you miss when you arrive (giant stepladders in case you're wondering!).

Once you have seen everything packed up in the van you have to take a deep breath ... and assume the worst! Then you can be pleasantly surprised at the other end when you are unpacking it all and it is all still in one piece.

7

Sailing Away

We arrived at the hotel which was to be our last night in the UK before sailing and discovered that we had booked into a hotel modelled on the television programme Fawlty Towers. It was described in the brochure online as 'posh' (for that read expensive) and we had decided to treat ourselves and have a decent place to stay. After all it was to be our last night on British soil for the foreseeable future. We opened the door to the room and gasped - it was the size of a shoe box. (Which at least made the comparison with the size of our cabin on the ferry once we saw it quite a positive thing!) Oh well, we thought, it's just a bed to sleep in, and we went off out for a quick meal.

That last meal was a quiet affair for both of us. We had said goodbye to our friends and family, and we were on our way. Visions of one of our dear friends, Suz, who had tears running down her face as she said goodbye to us as we drove away from her house after a final riotous meal together with her husband Adam and their two young children, was etched on my mind. Of course, you have doubts, it is a big decision to move abroad. But it was a bit late now, the van had been loaded, all our contracts and services had been cancelled, the flat we had rented in the UK had new occupants, so it was time to take a deep breath and move forward. I can honestly say that I can count on one hand the moments when I thought 'what have we done?' since we moved to Portugal. And the final night in Britain was no time to dwell on such things.

I had never sailed on a ferry before and so we changed the subject from leaving our friends behind and instead chatted about what it was going to be like on the ferry crossing. I could find very little information on this in advance. I had scoured websites and forums and asked lots of friends; and opinions ranged from 'I will never do that ferry crossing again as long as I live,' to 'It was lovely, very soporific'. We sailed on the Pont Aven from Plymouth to Santander, and even their own website was a bit basic and not very useful. We also managed to pick a day which had gale force winds forecast (oh joy!) and I am not exactly known for being a fan of boats and sailing at the best of times.

There are lots of things I wish I had known before we set sail. Let's put it another way - I will 'never' do the same journey again. Dave's view of the same trip: 'It wasn't that bad!'. You can tell which of us has sea legs from that comment. I wrote a list of things that I would give to someone as helpful advice should they be considering the same journey:

Book a cabin with a porthole window, or if you can splash out, a Commodore cabin with a balcony. Being able to see the horizon really helps when the boat starts pitching and rolling. Well that is what I kept telling myself as I stared out of the tiny window and saw the swell and waves moving in and out of view.

Crystallised ginger and travel calm tablets help a little. So does lying down on the bunk bed and groaning! (It was a pretty bumpy ride). Lying on the bed counting how many more hours, minutes and seconds are left of the journey does not help. Falling asleep into oblivion helps enormously.

If you ask a cabin crew member how the ride over was (they just tend to go back and forward on the same route all the time) and their reply is "so-so" you know you are in for some heaving swell ... their standard response is apparently "all fine, very good."

Eat as soon as you get on board, on the premise that if it is rough later at least you have eaten. Trust me eating is the last thing you will want to do if it does get rough and the cafés all shut quite early. If you want to dine á la carte you can (it is more expensive) and you have to queue up half an hour after they start sailing to secure a table (apparently you can book on line in advance - their website beat me here) but the thought of fine dining did not exactly appeal to me once we got moving. I curled up and went to sleep, trying not to think too much about where we were and what was happening outside that little porthole window.

Dave on the other hand, was fine. And starving hungry, so off he went to the main posh restaurant in the vague hope that he might get a little table in the corner all to himself. The boat lurched and heaved as he made his way around the corridors and stairs, however our intrepid hungry hero wasn't in the slightest bit perturbed and arrived at the entrance to the restaurant to be greeted by a French waiter who looked delighted to see him.

The reason why was evident the moment Dave stepped inside, and the waiter asked him where he would like to sit, and Dave realised that the entire room was empty of people. He was literally the only person there wanting to eat. Not one to disappoint the kitchen staff, he proceeded to order and scoff a hearty three course meal, and as he was polishing off the last of his dessert, the waiter approached him and asked him,

"Excuse me sir, were you in the Navy?!"

The cabin does have towels, but it is best to take your own toiletries with you. They provide a sachet of something smelly and showery that is about the size of a sugar sachet to be shared between two people. And if you need to go to the toilet, you need to 'back into' the cabin as there is no room whatsoever to turn around in there. Whoever designed them deserves a medal for ingenuity and resilience.

If you decide to pay extra to have all your worldly goods insured by the removal company that are bringing everything down to Portugal for you; it is worth finding out which ferry crossing they are going to be booked on. We were sat in the car queue waiting to board the ferry and then realised that the two guys cheerily waving at us from a delivery lorry in the next line beside us waiting to board were our delivery men. Our lorry with all our worldly goods on board was boarding the same ferry as us. This was also the moment when I wondered why we had bothered to pay for insurance. Presumably, I thought, if the ferry goes down with all you own in the world on board, but you are also sat in a cabin on board going down too, it's a bit pointless being insured!

In the space of 24 hours we went from speaking English, to pidgin French, to even worse Spanish, to basic Portuguese ... which was quite enough of a linguistic challenge for both of us for one day. Most people speak French on board the ferry, although you will be fine speaking English.

We woke in time to watch the ferry glide into Santander which was a very special moment. The water was as calm as a pond, the boat was moving smoothly, and it was as if the nightmare of the Bay of Biscay had never actually happened. We gathered up our things, grinned at each other and set off to find our car.

Finding your car once the ferry docks is fun! Going down into the depths of the boat after the bright sunshine of Santander was a shock, and we sat in the gloom waiting for the green light and the cars in front of us to move. And then suddenly we were out - and away.

Driving through Spain was quite easy, although our shiny new sat-nav had several blank moments on us, at it just didn't recognise huge swathes of new motorways that had been built, and it kept trying to direct us into tiny one shop one church villages, complete with horse drawn carts and bemused locals.

Spanish service stations almost deserve a chapter of their own - suffice to say that if you want to eat then you'll need to like sandwiches, including ones that are 'kebab' flavoured on stale flat bread. Next time we'll pack a picnic.

Finding Portugal is quite easy, just drive to Seville and turn right! We were very tired and happy when we finally saw the 'Welcome to Portugal' sign as we crossed the border into our new home country.

We had planned, dreamed about, and longed for, the exciting

moment when we would arrive in Ferragudo, coming 'home' to our lovely house, and start our new life here. The reality was far more down to earth; after eleven hours of driving we were shattered, we dumped our bags, had a glass of red wine, nibbled some digestive biscuits (no food in the fridge of course!) and then crashed into bed.

And woke up to the removal man ringing us very early the next morning to say,

"Can we deliver this morning, we're ready to come over?"

Our new life in Portugal was about to begin.

8

Settling In

We were finally waking up in our Algarve home. The first day of our new lives here in Portugal involved us scampering round getting ready for the removal men, who turned up bright and early, and far too cheerfully, and proceeded to start unloading the lorry with alarming speed. Within an hour, we had boxes everywhere, empty mugs on the kitchen counter, and the first of many empty packets of biscuits discarded.

By lunchtime the furniture was all in the house, the rooms were piled high with far too many boxes and packets, and we were officially 'in residence'. We had tried to plan the moment when we combined two homes of furniture and items quite carefully to avoid too much duplication. When we originally bought the house here, it was unfurnished, and we had the fun trip of travelling up to Ikea in Lisbon, armed with a very well organised list of items and furniture that we required. The shopping list was planned around the items we already had in the UK that we always intended to bring out with us when we finally moved here permanently.

In one day in Ikea, we managed to spend 7,000 euros and furnish a 4-bedroom house. We also discovered the fabulous Portuguese word *montagem* (to build or to assemble) when we came to pay and then organise the transport company to bring everything down to the Algarve. We had twelve trolleys piled high with 'small stuff' by the time we got to the tills at 1030 p.m. at night (they close at 11 p.m.) and that didn't include the 'heavy goods' that were 'somewhere in the back' ready for us to pick up. We walked over to the delivery section and the very helpful person behind the till asked us if we wanted to have the delivery items built as well on arrival at their destination.

"Really ... all of this - built?!" we asked.

Well it had to be worth the enquiry of how much they would charge us, and to this day we still smile when we recall the answer we received. 120 euros for everything to be delivered and built. We almost snatched the pen out of her hand in our eagerness to sign up before she changed her mind or realised that she had quoted us the wrong price!

Sure enough, a week later, a very large flat-bed lorry arrived outside our house, two nice friendly men jumped out and unloaded all the boxes and proceeded to build everything for us. Double beds, wardrobes, dining table and chairs, you name it, they built it in record time. By 5 p.m. the same day they had finished. It was quite amazing. They also raced each other to build a room, by selecting a room each piled high with flat-pack boxes and proceeded to see who could finish building the contents of their selected room first - unaided. I have never seen a person manage to build an Ikea wardrobe single-handed before.

We were pretty proficient at the removal and setting up home lark; having moved so many times for work in the UK, and this time around by the second day of full-time living in the Algarve, we were in and unpacked and pretty much sorted out. The furniture we had already bought at Ikea fitted in perfectly with all the smaller items that we had brought over from the UK with us.

We began to realise though that we had packed far too many unsuitable clothes for our new lifestyle out here and I quickly decided that my full-length ballgown was probably not required! (Seriously, what was I thinking, packing it in the first place?!) Goodness knows what the local charity shop thought when it opened the first of several bin bags full of clothes and other items and pulled out a burgundy taffeta full length ballgown.

We arrived in May, it was lovely and hot and sunny, and summer was just around the corner. All we needed were shorts, T-shirts and flip-flops. And lots of sun cream. And no ballgowns.

❖ 🝆 ❖ ❧ ❖

We began adjusting to a new speed and our new way of life.

I have always liked the quote by C.S. Lewis which states that: "The future is something which everyone reaches at the rate of sixty minutes an hour, whatever he does, whoever he is."

Although it does feel as if the Portuguese 'hour' has more than sixty minutes. How else would you manage to fit in all of those pauses for coffee and leisurely sit-downs, and still manage to get things done. Albeit perhaps a little more slowly than in the UK.

Setting up our phone line and internet when we arrived was a good example of the Portuguese art of slow efficiency and quirkiness. We visited a local showroom, but we could not get the deal we wanted without having to sign up to 140+ TV channels which we did not need or want. So we went online (that in itself is tricky if you don't actually have any internet yet!) and we found exactly what we needed - a package with a telephone line, email and broadband (with no TV). There was just one slight problem ... to book it online you needed to have ... a telephone number so that the company could call you!

Luckily, we already had a Portuguese mobile phone. A salesperson called my mobile phone and asked me to send them copies of our documentation including our address details which they said we had to send to them by email! So, for us to be able to book the internet and email package that we needed - we would need to have ... the internet and an email! We already had a wireless dongle and a UK email account (hello Sky - remember us!) so we used that to help us send them the information they needed via email. And then finally we had sent everything through, and three phone calls later, each time with a different person offering me a different package at a different price … we eventually had three men arriving at the front door of our house to connect our phone … and there the fun really began!

We ended up with all three men scratching their chins an hour later and staring into the large hole in the ground they had dug. They all scurried off, muttering the Portuguese equivalent of,

"Ooh sorry, no, we can't do that there … we'll need to send someone else round," whilst dramatically sucking in air through their teeth and shrugging wildly.

Eventually another man came along, with an impressive-looking metal briefcase and a testing kit and sorted out something technical in the road, and finally we had our internet and a phone line sorted out.

But days later we were still giggling over the fact that in order to be able to set up a phone line, email and internet over here … you will need to have already set yourself up with … a phone, email and the internet.

We also discovered an inverse proportion theory all our own. The smaller, quicker and easier an unpacking or building job seemed to be the longer it would take us to complete. We managed to build and unpack an entire room full of contents and furniture in one day, and yet the hanging of one small electric fire in the lounge took an entire day all on its own. I'm still not convinced it is straight, but that's another story!

We also found an interesting dilemma of still being on 'UK time' internally as we scurried around trying to unpack everything. It was a strange emotional balance between wanting to get things sorted and settled, and the excitement of finding new homes for our precious things and wanting to chill out and enjoy the gorgeous sunshine and slower pace of life.

In the first few days of arriving though we took time to rediscover the simple pleasures that we loved. We enjoyed a leisurely paddle in the waves at sunset on our local beach; found a huge punnet of strawberries in our local supermarket for 79 cents and ate tomatoes that tasted like proper tomatoes. We sauntered down to the square to our favourite café for a morning coffee and strolled back down there in the late afternoon for yet another coffee.

We also lost count of the number of times we went back to our local Continente supermarket to buy more UK plug adapters - seriously how many plugs can the electricity supply to one house sustain?

And we had a new wi-fi router with lots of flashing green lights, and a new telephone line to play with. Of course, nothing is that easy, so we had a router which did not reach our computer and an explanation that we needed to go to the shop to buy a 'pen' for the wi-fi ... if only our understanding of the Portuguese language was better! We did of course eventually manage to sort everything out. It took a while though.

And then suddenly we had been living in our new home for two months, and according to friends our honeymoon phase should have been reaching an end. It is apparently common to suddenly drop emotionally once the high of moving has worn off and you may start to feel a little deflated or tired. Well that wasn't us - that was just all our appliances! In the first two months all of the following things wore out or stopped working on us: the microwave oven; the George Foreman Grill (which didn't make it past round six!); the orange juice presser thingy; the much better half's power drill (a bit essential for us with all the DIY we had been doing); the updated Skype programme on the computer (which was essential!) (we downloaded the update and it was fine again) and much to Dave's consternation and horror - and the final straw - the espresso coffee machine packed up!

We then had the fun of the builders arriving with a giant cement-mixing machine to lay a concrete drive and patio for us, and we watched with some consternation as a giant mechanical feeder arm stretched itself from the main road right over the top roof of our house and into the back garden, and began spewing tons of wet concrete onto the ground. The builder's team worked like fury to level it all as it landed and they did a fabulous job. We finally had the 'easy to maintain' garden we were hoping for.

Sadly the plumber's brilliant work in our basement to set up the washing machine and sink was slightly marred by the discovery a week later that the manhole cover and drain in the corner of the room didn't connect to anything. It is amazing how much water a washing machine can churn out onto the basement floor! We had to have part of the new drive dug up and new drainage pipes laid.

But we carried on smiling through it all. How could we not smile with such amazing sunny weather and our fabulous home to enjoy. It was amazing to realise how much our lives had changed for the better, we were definitely starting to find out that a simpler life has so many benefits, and we were also amazed by how quickly we felt that we had settled down and felt at home with our new life here.

9

Meeting the Locals

We chose to live amongst a local Portuguese community on purpose. I have got nothing against expat enclaves as such, but we didn't want to move to a gated community and feel isolated from a real way of life, and one of the things that we love most about living in Portugal is the Portuguese people and their simple way of life. All our neighbours are Portuguese and greet us warmly whenever they see us.

One of them, António, chats to us enthusiastically every time he sees us. He is our local neighbourhood watch, he is always wandering around the local houses and streets, watching everything that happens. He is a retired gardener from a posh hotel, and he doesn't miss a trick. If there is a hole being dug in the road (we seem to have that happen a lot round here!) António will be there leaning over the edge of the pit, ready with words of advice and help. I'm not sure what the workmen make of him and his elaborate gems of wisdom, and I doubt he knows much about hole-digging apart from the kind of hole that you dig to plant a tree ... but he is always there to lend a proverbial verbal hand!

When we first met him, we were attempting to plant something green and leafy in pots to enhance the concrete and tiles that surround our house, and he would lean over the gate and give helpful advice in Portuguese to us. Mostly that actually consisted of him telling us that what we were planting was in the wrong place, or in the wrong pot, or that we were planting at the wrong time of day (never plant before 5 p.m.) or often ... all the above!

He turned up one afternoon with a stack of plastic plant pots having told us that the expensive ceramic ones we had bought were not suitable for what we were doing. He was also clutching a sack of something resembling old bones and fishmeal. To this day I still don't know what it was, but he patiently showed us how to mix this into the compost for our plants. It is little gestures like that, and the frequent bags of lemons and fruit that we find hanging on our front door handle, that confirm for us that we have chosen the right place to live.

António has also given us our fair share of funniest neighbour moments too. He must be in his late seventies, and when we met him, he only had two or three front teeth in his head. We had got used to trying to understand his Portuguese which was accompanied by the sucking and whistling sounds of his remaining teeth, and we had grown quite fond of his particular brand of language and even managed to understand quite a bit of what he was saying. I am not sure what that says about our understanding of the local language however! One day that all changed though, when we saw him leaning over our gate to say good morning to us. We had such a shock as he had been to the dentist and had been fitted with a new set of teeth top and bottom! Not only that but we think he must have secretly flown to America to get his teeth made, as they were a gleaming Hollywood white, and seemed to shine rather brightly in the sun. We both said "whoa!" and took a step backwards when we saw them for the first time.

Sadly, he has never really got the hang of talking with his new set of teeth and we can now barely understand him. I miss the old toothless version of António!

He is also fiercely loyal to Portugal too as we found out when we introduced him to our little rescue dog who had been abandoned in Spain and is a version of a Spanish water dog. He was very animated when he first saw her, crouching down and fussing her until I mentioned the crucial fact that she is Spanish. He promptly stood up, did the 'wiping of the hands' demonstration that Europeans do so well as a visual brush-off, and then walked off muttering! Poor Kat, our little dog, I guess her integration and acceptance by the locals into a foreign country is going to take a while!

❖෨◊ℚ❖

Our lack of green fingers and leafy objects probably amuses all our neighbours. Everyone around us seems to be able to grow things better than us, which wasn't helped by the fact that for several years after buying the house we would leave it unoccupied for several months at a time. It is not conducive to growing anything in this hot climate as we found out the hard way. Initially we tried to dig out and plant a couple of small flowerbeds in the front garden, which is when we discovered that the 'soil' we had in our garden was rather different to the British soil we were used to. It was also probably not helped by the fact that we think that our house was the last to be built and finished in the street, and that our plot was obviously the dumping ground for everyone else's rubble and rubbish. Well that would at least explain what we were digging up anyway! We bought normal garden tools from a local garden centre, and within 10 minutes of starting to dig and watching the handles bend and the ends of the tools break off in the 'soil' we realised we had met our match.

Along came another neighbour, this time a kind and gentle man aged almost eighty, who lives nearby. He took one look at us over the garden gate, shook his head, wandered off and came back a few minutes later with what can only be described as a giant double-ended pickaxe about four foot long. He handed it over to Dave who manfully started swinging it at the ground, much to the amusement of the neighbour who stood watching in the blazing sunshine. Now Dave is no slouch and he can hold his own with the best of them, but this tool was rather awesomely proportioned and very heavy. And obviously Dave just wasn't doing it right, as the neighbour strolled into the garden, took the medieval tool out of Dave's hands and proceeded to swing it right over his head and down into the soil. The fact he was almost thirty years older than Dave didn't factor into it at all, and he spent a good ten minutes swinging and crashing it into the ground, before handing it back to Dave. And I swear I saw a gleam in his eyes as he did so!

He then returned an hour later with an armful of plants for us to place in the newly tilled soil. Sadly, despite all our best efforts, the next time we returned to the house after another spell back at work in the UK, we were greeted by a wilting dead mass of green stalks and brown shoots that were once plants. And a neighbour that still looks over the gate and shakes his head at us in amusement and probably wonders why we ever tried to plant things there.

It is also not helped by our immediate neighbour who has a small market garden of fruit and vegetables all thriving and growing wildly and abundantly over the fence from us. So far, we have successfully managed to tend to a tiny lemon tree in a pot which has given us several batches of fruit, a sad but barely still alive bougainvillea plant and a hefty selection of dandelions.

We even have fake grass in the back garden which I am quite sure is a source of great amusement to our neighbours. We gave up on the idea of a vegetable plot, for obvious reasons, and decided that the best thing we could do would be to cover the area with something easy to manage. The fake grass is at least green all year round and requires zero watering. And from a distance - the distance António and his teeth are from our front wall - it probably looks reasonably ok.

✧ℬ✧ℜ✧

We have been blessed with some wonderful, kind, gentle neighbours who have given us so many lemons and other fruit that we sometimes find ourselves clutching an extremely full carrier bag already crammed full of fruit whilst our neighbour continues to load us up with more lemons! It almost seems such a waste to just use them in a cold jug of water, so we often make home-made lemonade. (Sssh!

Don't tell anyone how much sugar we add!) I keep promising to look up some new recipes with lemons or oranges in them so if anyone out there has any recipes they can recommend, please do share them with us!

Even when we rented the small fisherman's cottage in the village our old neighbour there used to greet us with home-made traditional marzipan cakes, all laid out on a plate ready to eat and they were delicious. It is obviously a Portuguese tradition to feed up scrawny (and not so scrawny!) English neighbours.

Our neighbour's daughter recently graduated from University and they have a quaint custom of wearing ribbons on their gowns for their graduation ceremony which have been decorated by friends and family. We learnt that the family traditionally decorate a white ribbon and friends get a very nice dark blue colour. We were honoured when we were asked to decorate a ribbon for her to wear proudly on her special day.

Whilst I was busy painting the ribbon in the studio, our neighbour called us over and handed us a plate full of steaming hot freshly barbecued sardines for lunch. Now that's what I call a fair exchange!

Their generosity even extended to New Year's Eve on our first New Year that we spent here. We were happily sat on our balcony at midnight watching the local fireworks (we do have a pretty good ringside seat from where we are!) and we were then cajoled to climb over the adjoining wall and join them next door. We then sat learning to play a very ancient family board game whilst being offered plates of food and lots to drink. I think we got home again about 4.30 a.m. after a most enjoyable time.

✿ ✾ ✿ ✽ ✿

We have met so many gentle and kind people who seem to go out of their way to help us. Two examples spring to mind:

We love one of our local restaurants called Toc-Toc and especially their caramel mousse dessert. Sílvia, the owner, knows this, as I always try to surreptitiously lick the bowl clean (with my finger!) when she is not looking (and I usually get caught!). The wonders of the modern Facebook world meant that they discovered that it was my birthday and at about 9.30 p.m. that night there was a knock on the door. I opened the door and it was Luís from the restaurant clutching an enormous glass bowl full of caramel mousse for me. It was so big it took us three nights to polish it all off (and believe me I had a very good go at it!) and I was so surprised and delighted by such a lovely gesture.

We also have a lovely local shop in the village that sells crafts, vases, gifts, pottery, well, you name it, Salomé probably sells it. We've nicknamed her shop 'new stock Wednesdays' as it is a running joke that if you cannot find something you like she will always tell you she has more stock coming on Wednesday. I have no idea where she puts it all in her little Aladdin's cave. We bought quite a few things from her when we first bought our house as we were determined to buy local whenever possible.

On one occasion we had purchased quite a few small glass and vase items, and a large discount was immediately given; and then each item was beautifully and painstakingly wrapped with lovely paper, ribbons and bows. We paid her and she then left her shop completely open and unattended and helped us carry all the packages to our car which was parked on the other side of the village square.

Sometimes you feel as if you have stepped back fifty years in time, to a land almost forgotten, whilst living here, which is not always a bad thing.

The kindness and genuine welcome we have been shown here is something special. Maybe it is because we live in a relatively small and unspoilt village, perhaps it is because we have all local Portuguese neighbours, or maybe it is in part due to our willingness to meet new people, learn new ways, and try our best to immerse ourselves in a different culture and way of life. Whatever the reasons, the Portuguese people are a very special and treasured part of our lives here.

10

The Famous and not so Famous

There are many famous faces around the Algarve, Sir Cliff Richard and Bonnie Tyler are regulars here and can often be spotted out and about, along with many others who have holiday homes here in the Algarve. One of the most famous Portuguese names must be José Mourinho, football coach and local legend. José Mourinho's father, José Manuel Mourinho Félix, was born in Ferragudo, and José Junior often travels back to Ferragudo having bought a home himself on the edge of town.

One of our favourite local cafés, sadly now an Italian take-away, was run by the cheeky João and his wife Marina, who became good friends of ours. We regularly visited them for a morning coffee or lunch, so that we could sit in the square and watch the world pass by. One morning we popped in and we were greeted by an extremely happy João, who was pinning up a photograph on the wall behind the counter of himself stood next to José Mourinho.

We teased him about the illustrious company he was keeping, and he proudly told us that José was a regular at the café.

"Oh yes, of course he is," we replied, not believing him at all.

"No, he is, he is, I will prove it to you!" João replied.

We were not convinced, which was not helped by the fact that on the next two occasions we went into the café, João would say,

"Did you see him, José, he was here, he left not five minutes ago?!"

We continued to tease him, not believing a word of it of course.

Another morning went by and we went down to the square for a coffee, the café was unusually busy, and I just managed to squeeze into a chair at a table in front of another table with four men who were seated and chatted animatedly. I have rather long legs, especially for Portugal, and I had to literally push my chair back almost onto the back of the chair behind me in order to sit down. Dave and I sat and chatted, had coffee, the table behind us left, and I went in to pay João.

"Did you see him, Senhor José?" he said straight away.

"No, João, I didn't see him," I said with a sigh, thinking, 'Oh dear, this is getting boring now!'

"But he was sat right behind you, at the next table. You did not recognise him?" he said.

"Erm, no!" I said falteringly.

I went away thinking perhaps he was telling the truth, after all the man sat behind me did have a rather fabulous aftershave on, I couldn't help but notice that!!

The mystery was finally solved the following morning when we returned to the café, and there sat at a table in the sunshine, relaxed, tanned and hiding rather unsuccessfully under a baseball cap, was the man himself, José Mourinho. We had no intention of bothering him, and the locals all seemed unconcerned; however, João was having none of it, and came bounding out of the café, gleefully introducing us to 'his friend José' with a knowing grin.

We admitted defeat and chatted to them both; and agreed that José was a very nice man in person, and confirmed that he was wearing a fabulous aftershave ... I just didn't have the nerve to ask him what it was called! And from that day, we had to concede that João did indeed have a rather famous friend.

❀⊱✿⊰❀

In any village or town there is, rather inevitably, an expat contingent that likes to socialise together. Whilst I have nothing against them personally; and we have made some lovely British friends along the way; it has never really appealed to me to move abroad to a new culture and place and then end up spending all my time with British people.

Having local people that we can class as friends is important to us, learning about their different ways, their culture, humour and different traditions is fascinating, and humbling too. Watching a man fishing on the end of the pier and seeing the few small fish in his bucket, knowing that that will be dinner for him and his family that day, makes you question the shopping trolley full of food you later push around the local supermarket. I'm not sure who would be envious of who at that moment.

The expat socialite parties certainly ensure that someone pushes a full trolley of food and drink around the supermarket beforehand; that is unless they bring in a private catering firm of course. We had always strenuously denied all invitations of that nature, until one day someone we were acquainted with in the village insisted that we came to her 'little gathering' that evening. With nothing planned, and no fish in our proverbial bucket planned for dinner that evening, we said yes, and gathered up the directions to her house. 'How bad can it be?' we thought to ourselves, privately agreeing that if it was indeed awful, we would make our excuses and beat a hasty retreat.

We arrived to hear music playing, there were fairy lights and lanterns strewn around the garden, and the ubiquitous catering company was in place handing round canapés on small silver platters. The food, at least, was good, as we stood eating and staring around us at the hoard of - all British - people, stood chatting and laughing. 'Oh well, here goes' I thought and went over to chat to someone I vaguely recognised.

I probably should warn you at this point that Dave's sense of humour begins somewhere close to Monty Python, and veers over into the Spike Milligan field. Add in a liberal dose of John Cleese in Fawlty Towers, and you've found Dave. I left him to mingle which with hindsight might have been a bit brave of me – but not for him!

He is the master of the art of extricating himself from someone he doesn't want to talk to; I'm usually the one stood wishing I could move away from the person I've been stuck listening to, as they tell me some faintly ridiculous or boring story whilst simultaneously picking their teeth with a cocktail stick. Oh dear.

After about half an hour I glanced round and spotted Dave chatting to a group of three women who were all listening rather avidly. There was a moment when all three of them recoiled slightly and then hurried away; one of them scurried straight over to the host nearby and started talking to her, pointing over at Dave. 'Oh no, I thought, what has he said now?!'

I sauntered over and saw Dave grinning away to himself which is never a good sign.

"What did you say to them?" I said, knowing he had said something controversial.

"Oh well, I got bored of answering the same questions over and over," came his reply.

"What questions?" I said.

"You know, the 'what is your name and what do you do?' questions that everyone here asks you."

"Yes fine, but what did you say to those three you were chatting to?"

It transpires that one of the three had asked Dave if he lived here in Ferragudo, to which he had replied that he did.

"Oh no, you can't live here all the time," she had replied, "you're far too pale to live here."

We are not great sun worshippers, and neither of us can just sit in the sun and do nothing, so even in summer we are not the brownest creatures on the planet. I tend to turn pink then red then white anyway, so we have more of a 'slow-burn' approach to sunbathing if you'll pardon the pun. Dave had been busy with lots of photography work and that tends to ensure he isn't that bronzed, but this lady obviously took exception to Dave not having a leathery brown suntan.

Dave's reply to this certainly hit the mark. He sized her up, sighed deeply and then said to her,

"Well, you won't tell anyone will you …" (a fatal blow to someone who was obviously being nosey) … and then he continued,

"but the reason I'm not very suntanned is that I have only just got out of prison in the UK."

"Oh!" she replied, and looked a bit flustered, but before she could say any more, Dave had continued,

"Yes, I've just been released, I served my time. I killed my wife you know."

The host sidled up to us a while later, and smiled at us, saying,

"I hear you've been having fun winding up my guests. Everyone keeps asking me to point out the wife-murderer to them."

Well, it certainly livened up a boring evening.

We didn't think we would be asked back again by the hosts, but they are obviously keen to liven up these events with some free entertainment and we were invited back to a similar social evening a few months later. This time I warned Dave not to tell anyone about his murderous past again (!) and to try not wind people up, but the mood obviously got the better of him. I spotted him chatting to a small group who were enthralled, and I thought 'oh dear, now what is he up to?' and sauntered over, just in time to catch him say the brilliant lines,

"Oh yes, I'm an emergency taxidermist. I get called out in the middle of the night to stuff dead animals; I even have a special green light I can put on top of my car to ensure I get there quickly."

I left him to it …

✿ဢ✿ଔ✿

One of Dave's finest moments must be the night we were invited to a local beach bar to celebrate the owner's birthday. Diane was celebrating a significant birthday, and we were delighted on this occasion to be invited to the private 'invite only' party. We sat chatting to the guests, many of whom were Portuguese and local to the village and known to us. The wine flowed, the food was laid out and everyone was in a festive mood.

Dave loves meeting new people and chatting to them and was

soon sat next to someone we didn't know, talking animatedly about the world and the local gossip with a fascinating man. After an hour or so, the conversation moved on to what we all did for a living, of course, and Dave's new friend, Barry, modestly said that he was a songwriter.

They chatted on for a while, and Dave discovered that Barry was in fact Diane's brother. Dave casually said to him,

"So, have you written anything I might know then?" not wanting to offend Barry.

"Oh possibly," he replied.

"Go on then, name something and I'll see if I know it," said Dave obligingly.

"Well, I wrote 'Delilah' for Tom Jones; and 'The Last Waltz' ... oh, and quite a few other hits too."

Barry Mason, we discovered, was rather famous. He was also utterly charming and great company.

11

Learning the Language

I did try to learn some Portuguese before we settled here, and numerous holidays and trips to our house certainly gave us the basics; particularly as I often found myself repeating the same words and phrases on each holiday. I am always willing to try to speak Portuguese though, often with hilarious results, as you are about to discover.

I have had plenty of CDs and computer programmes to choose from over the years; however sadly the best one for me is still a pre-school level computer programme that matches words and pictures at such a basic level that a small child could probably render the whole package as obsolete in a few weeks.

I am however quite good at giving directions now which is quite useful when a delivery van wants to find our house. Several years previously I had set our UK car's satnav system to speak Portuguese to me as I drove around the towns and villages of Devon for work each day. I was late for many appointments.

However nothing really prepares you for the linguistic onslaught that is a local Algarvian in full swing pelting you with unfamiliar words. They often sound strangely angry even though they are smiling broadly at you. We have discovered that arm waving and sign language is a must if you want to get by out here.

The other barrier to learning is that the locals are so helpful out here and so many people want to speak English to you, and are so accommodating, that it doesn't help you to practice and learn your adopted language. Portuguese friends in the tourist sector have also said to us that it is actually easier and quicker for them to speak to foreign people in English rather than wait for us to try and stutter and stumble over words in Portuguese to them, particularly in the summer months when they are at their busiest. Being rubbish at languages when I was at secondary school doesn't help me, and finding that, some words aside, Portuguese is closer to Latin and Russian than it is to Spanish is also a shock. If only I had learnt Latin at school or paid more attention in my French lessons.

We have found that there are so many languages spoken here, and there are people from all over the world who live and work here. We now have Dutch, Canadian, Icelandic, Belgium and Polish friends here ... all of whom also speak better Portuguese than us.

'What time of day is it anyway?' is now one of my favourite silly phrases. One of the things I decided as soon as I arrived here was that I would no longer wear a watch. My whole working life had revolved around the time; what time was the next meeting, how long am I going to be driving for, or sat in my car not moving on the M25 car park, what time will I get home tonight, and so on. I was determined that life out here would not revolve around hours and minutes, and my watch was ditched in favour of some colourful yarn and a few ethnic style bracelets. After about a month of not having a clue what time it was and glancing at my wrist every time I thought I needed to know the time, I relaxed and I could more or less work out the time, which seemed sufficient.

After a couple more weeks of relaxing into our new way of life though I was struggling to know which day of the week it was, let alone what time it was, and Dave was not fairing much better. Our standard retort to each other was always 'Is it Tuesday?' ... well living out here seems to have that effect on you. I think I might have taken this relaxed way of life too far at the point where the conversation with Dave went along these lines,

Me: "Is it Tuesday today?"

Dave: "No it's Wednesday."

Me: "Oh I thought it was Tuesday. Oh well at least I know the month, it's June."

Dave: "Actually it's not, it's July. It's been July for about a week now."

Whoops!

The other constant source of amusement and confusion, even after many years of living here and a lot more years on top of that of holidaying here, is how to greet someone you meet – whatever day of the week it is. There is a fine art to this and one I fear I will never master. The guidebooks make this sound so easy, in the morning you say *bom dia* (good morning); in the afternoon you say *boa tarde* (good afternoon) and at night you say *boa noite* (good night). Well that all sounds quite simple and easy to remember. Or ... not so simple. The morning is easy, *bom dia* rolls off the tongue, no problem.

Then at midday it gets a little trickier. Portuguese friends reliably informed us that midday is the crunch point, as soon as the clock bongs, it's time to change to *boa tarde*. Except you gleefully greet someone here at 12.01 p.m. with *boa tarde* and they smile at you and say *bom dia* in return. Or better you think 'ah-ha it's past 12 o'clock but I know that really you're still going to say *bom dia* to me' ... so you greet them with *bom dia* and they shake their head at you and say *boa tarde* in a very knowingly complacent kind of way. Of course, not wearing a watch doesn't help!

And then other Portuguese friends told us,

"Oh no it depends on whether you have had your lunch ... after lunch we say *boa tarde*."

So in order to get this right when you meet someone, you must first have a look at their midriff to try to decide if they have eaten or not before you speak to them. Do they have any tell-tale crumbs on their jumper, or a slightly satisfied 'full belly' kind of look to them? My advice is to dive in with a hastily muttered *boa tarde* and hope for the best.

The only other way of ensuring you are getting this right is of course to wait for them to speak to you first but being British and wanting to try to speak Portuguese means you are often the first one to speak. *Boa noite* isn't much easier to judge either, as you use it 'when it is dark'. Which out here can mean anything from after 5 p.m. in the winter; to still saying *boa tarde* to someone at about 10 p.m. in the summer. And what about when it is 'dimpsy' as they say in the West Country in the UK, that twilight half-dark time when it's not quite dark yet? It is a tricky business this learning a new language lark!

It is also weird saying 'good-night' to someone as a form of greeting when you meet them and say hello. In the UK that is how you would say 'good-bye' to someone as you are leaving; but here it is used a lot, it is a way of acknowledging someone, or saying hello, and with the right nod of the head it can mean a whole 'hello, how are you, nice to see you again, goodbye' all in one!

And if you walk your dog early enough in the morning, you can be saying *bom dia* to someone in the winter when it is still dark. Apparently 7 a.m. is the magic moment when day begins and night ends even if it is still dark all around you. I had a lady one morning who waited patiently after I had said *boa noite* to her until the church clock had chimed its seven morning chimes. She then tipped her head towards the church, nodded knowingly at me and said *bom dia* with a smile that verged on being a tad smug.

It is also not helped by the Algarvian knack of local people shortening absolutely everything they say to its bluntest form. All I hear is *'tarde'* or *'noite'* and if you ask *'como está?'* (how are you?) to someone, what I hear as the reply is just *'bem'* (good) or even just *'tudo'* (everything). I spent ages thumbing through my little English-Portuguese dictionary trying to look up the word 'da' and not getting anywhere as I kept hearing 'da'bom' or 'da'bay' when someone replied to me. What they were actually saying to me was *'está è bom'* (I am well) or *'está è bem'* (I am good). You hear people answer their phone with the word 'doh' and at that point I give up and just copy them, with no real idea what I am saying.

The problems don't end as soon as you start learning a few words and phrases. Having a basic grasp of about six verbs and a decent handful of basic words is worse than not having any words at all. You start a simple conversation in Portuguese, and the person will reply to you in either Portuguese or English. If you reply to them again in Portuguese, they will assume that you are quite fluent and will reply to you in rapid fire Portuguese that you have no hope of ever understanding.

The Portuguese speak quickly. Very quickly. It has become a game now; can I reply in Portuguese and will they reply to me in Portuguese again? If I can manage a whole conversation in the same language, then I feel like I have won a small, but still significant, linguistic victory. Never mind that I probably sound like a five-year-old at school tripping over the pronunciation and grammar of every word.

It is also not helped by the fact that one of the main sounds out here ... the *ão* sound ... is an impossible feat for me to accomplish. It has a sort of nasal groan that beats me every time. Friends have told me that the best way of perfecting this sound is to place a finger on each side of your nose and press gently, and then try to pronounce the sound. It works great but isn't really the thing to do in public!

As a painter that completes pet portraits as one of my themes this *ão* sound is quite a problem for me, as the word for dog in Portuguese is *cão*. My neighbour used to delight in asking me what I was painting, and I would reply *"um cão"*, and he would smile and 'moo' at me and say "oh a cow" in English. My reply of *"não uma vaca, um cão"* (not a cow a dog) with an accompanying "woof woof" must have made our other neighbours wonder what on earth was going on with all the moo-ing and woof-ing noises emitting from our garden. The word for a female dog however is a *cadela* and I can manage to say that quite easily. I am probably the only Pet Portrait artist here on the Algarve that only paints female dogs.

12

When Language Goes Wrong

I admit that if I am trying to ask about something technical or complicated in a shop I will usually ask if they speak English (at least I can ask that in fluent Portuguese) and if the phone rings at home it is nearly always cold-callers so I am very quick to pretend that I cannot speak any Portuguese at all (!) as that quickly sends them on their way and the phone goes dead. Not being fluent does have some advantages.

Speaking on the phone in Portuguese is much harder than in person and it makes you realise just how much you rely on sign language and arm signals when your arms are rendered obsolete.

A while ago I helped a local Portuguese friend to learn to speak better English as he works in the hotel trade and his English is actually very good, but his accent is very awkward. Like many Portuguese who have learnt their English mainly from the television, and often American television, their accent is often strained and unnatural. This teaching duty helped me with my Portuguese as well, and really tested me too. My qualified teacher status is a distant memory and my teaching days seem a very long time ago (although I am a qualified English teacher) so I often had to do my own homework the night before I met with him. How exactly do I describe prepositions and how can I teach them? And what are the 44 sounds of the English language?

In return, he helped me with pronouncing some difficult Portuguese words too and now I can finally pronounce where we live. I have always had a thing about trying to say the Portuguese word *urbanização* (urbanisation) which is awkward when it is in the first line of your own address. You would be surprised how many times you are asked for your address in Portugal. So now ... finally ... I can say it properly ... 'oo – ban – knee – za – saow'. And yes, I know, it's got one of those dreaded *ão* sounds at the end too.

His finest phrase was one that had me chortling with glee inside. Every week he greets new guests that arrive at the hotel, and gives them the same speech, telling them about the hotel and the local area. It includes the sentence,

"We have a beautiful beach here; you really must visit our beach."

All fine ... except that he was pronouncing 'beach' as 'bitch'. Oh dear, that won't help the tourism trade locally. Although, then again, perhaps it will!

It is not just the pronunciation though that can cause problems. Regardless of how well I think I have learnt to pronounce a word, that doesn't really help you when you get the word wrong in your head in the first place.

I popped into our local Lidl supermarket with a friend one afternoon and she managed to accidentally knock over two bottles of red wine which smashed all over the floor. Not wanting to just abandon the mess (which made an almighty loud smashing noise and spread red wine all over the floor), we waited around for the shop assistant whom we assumed must surely come rushing over (it was a very loud crash!) ... but nobody came. After a few minutes I thought 'I can do this, I can go to the till and get someone to help' so I wandered off to the tills, thinking through the simple Portuguese sentence I would need. I decided that I could manage to say,

"I have a problem with wine on the floor ... please can you help me?" (whilst gesturing towards the wine aisle).

To my knowledge, they don't have any staff that speak English in the store, so I did my best in halting Portuguese and was somewhat surprised at the reaction I received which was a very dismissive huff and wave of the hand by the assistant I spoke to. I wandered back to the wine mess on the floor and after about another five minutes we gave up waiting. I couldn't understand why no-one had come to help us. It wasn't until much later that I realised that what I had actually said was,

"I have a problem with wine on the ceiling."

They must have thought here comes a 'mad English alcoholic woman' and just ignored me.

I often end up getting words the wrong way around, or almost getting the right word but not quite. Our local café has the lovely bright parasol beer umbrellas outside that all cafés are blessed with here, but sadly they are usually only hoisted up to the height of the owner's father, and he is not exactly tall.

I managed to crash into one with my head the other morning and skipped into the café still laughing and rubbing my forehead.

"What is wrong?" asked the owner.

"Oh, your wardrobe is too small for my head," I gleefully replied.

An easy mistake to make, there is a *guarda-sol* (sun umbrella) and a *guarda-roupa* (wardrobe) and they have a *guard-chuva* (rain umbrella) too if it rains. What was most disconcerting is that it took me over 24 hours to realise that I had used the wrong *guarda* word; luckily for me our local café owner is quite used to my pained attempts at early morning Portuguese conversation and he didn't even bat an eyelid.

He does seem to enjoy stitching me up too. I sometimes use the little tiny saucer that accompanies an espresso coffee to pour some water into if I am out on a walk and I have forgotten Kat's water bowl. I popped in for a drink one day and ordered a cold drink for myself and then realised that the glass would not come with the saucer I needed. I went back inside and all that I could think to ask for in Portuguese was a 'small plate'. Eventually the owner realised what I wanted and pointed to the small saucers.

"Yes, one of those please," I said.

He replied that it was called a *'pides'* in Portuguese (well I thought that was what he said!) ... pronounced 'pee-des' (it turns out he was saying *pires* which shows how bad my ears are at hearing words properly!). The next afternoon I popped in there again, and his mother was working behind the counter, with several of her elderly friends sat around enjoying their afternoon rest. I proudly went up and asked for a 'pee-des' except of course I got it a bit wrong, and it came out more like 'pee-nes'. Yes, you've guessed it, I went up and asked his mom and all her friends if I could have a "small penis please." Oh dear!

〇🐚〇ℛ〇

My finest moment so far though must be when we had our house painted. It is a semi-detached house and when the outside needed painting we pitched in with our neighbour and had both houses painted the same colour at the same time. He knew a Portuguese decorator and it was all arranged.

Dear Joaquim, the painter, arrived and spoke no English at all. We got by with lots of gestures and fast thumbing through the dictionary to look up words like 'gable end' and 'undercoat'. He was an absolute delight to have working for us, he was polite, quiet, efficient and I have never seen anyone take such a quiet pride in their work as he did. He also did a fantastic job.

He was a creature of habit too; he arrived at 8.30 a.m. every morning, had a coffee at 11 a.m. packed up at 12.30 p.m. for lunch and returned at 2 p.m. On the first afternoon at 4 p.m. we offered him an ice-cream, and that became a daily habit for us to offer him an ice-cream of some description. He was a stickler for timing though, as we found out on the third day as we tried to hand him an ice-cream at 3.30 p.m. as we were going out. I managed to understand the gist of the ensuing Portuguese reply, which was along the lines of,

"But it's not 4 p.m. yet, please can you come back at 4 with my ice-cream. Thank you."

We had to wait to go out until after 4 p.m. that day.

At exactly 5 p.m. every day we all sat and had a cold beer together as he showed us what he had painted that day and explained what he would be painting the next day. He also learnt one English phrase in the three weeks he was there; the solitary but endearing 'bye-bye' that he said every day to us as he left, covered in paint, waving and smiling broadly.

A few months later when we looked at our internal three floors of hall, stairs and landing that needed painting; even though we had happily tackled all the rest of the DIY and painting ourselves, only one name sprang to mind. This time we happily left our neighbour with the keys and with instructions for Joaquim of what needed painting, and he told us that we could pay him next time we were out as we were still only holidaying at the house at the time.

And this is when the most embarrassing moment of my Portuguese life (so far) happened. It was all going so well up to that point too. We had arrived back at the house for another quick trip; the paint job inside was superb; and it was the moment when I had to call Joaquim to arrange to pay him.

Speaking on the phone is so much harder than in person; no arm waving or facial expressions can help you out; and I had carefully googled all the phrases I needed and written them down phonetically to help me pronounce them. Armed with all this research what could possibly go wrong?

I called him up and what I thought I said to him was,

"Hello, this is Alyson from Bela Vista. You have done a great job; I need to pay you, can you come to the house tomorrow so that I can pay you?"

There was a long pause, and a funny sound that I couldn't really make out, then Joaquim replied in Portuguese,

"Yes, I can come at 5 p.m. tomorrow. See you then." He quickly hung up.

I turned to Dave and he said,

"How did it go?" and I replied,

"Fine, he's coming here tomorrow at 5 p.m."

Off we went out to our friends' restaurant for the evening with me feeling rather smug at my little phone call. Our friends are Portuguese, but Helena speaks very good English, so we were telling her about my new prowess on the telephone and she said to me,

"Tell me what you said to him then?"

I rattled off my little sentences again feeling rather proud of myself.

Helena started laughing hysterically and shouted over to her husband from the kitchen to join us. She said something to him in rapid and excited Portuguese at which point he started laughing as well; in the end they were both holding each other up they were laughing so much.

I kept saying to them,

"What, what have I said?"

It took her several minutes to stop guffawing with laughter long enough to explain to me that what I had actually said to him was,

"Hello, this is Alyson from Bela Vista. I would like to give you a blow-job; and I will pay you, can you come to the house tomorrow?"

Needless to say; when 5 p.m. came the following day, I was nowhere to be seen when Joaquim arrived, and I left Dave to pay the poor man.

13

Trying to be Legal

R esidency is a strange concept to many people here, but we wanted to sleep easily at night, pay our taxes and be true members of the community and country that we have chosen to live in. It doesn't make us any less British ... just more legal and responsible. We also wanted to promote and run our own businesses here and setting those up properly was important to us.

We had heard horror stories of how difficult people had found gaining residency could be. The process involved stacks of paperwork and photocopies of everything in triplicate, with the obligatory staple in the top left corner of course.

We were so grateful for Ben and Louise from the 'Moving to Portugal' blog and book of the same name[1], not only because their book covered their trials and tribulations of gaining residency in Portugal; but also because they were brave enough to say 'we want to do this properly' and live legally as well. The number of people who told us 'not to bother' and to just live 'under the radar' was ridiculous, and we were treated with more than a little disdain and even outright hostility by some people, because we dared to do things properly.

When we look back on it now, we realise that we had quite a

painless and easy experience gaining the illustrious *residência* papers (sorry Ben and Louise!) but please bear in mind this was just our experience. We were covered by the Lagoa town council and they seemed to have things organised and were very efficient. We obviously cannot tell you what another town might be like, as each one seems to have a different approach. We can however recommend having lots of coffees and pastries to help you through the process.

The first thing I did was lots of research online but to be honest, looking back on it, I wish I hadn't bothered! Every website I read told me something different and each site listed a different set of forms and identification which was required. After a morning of research I gave up and thought we would just 'go for it' and work it out as we went along.

It is officially called the *'Certificado de Registo de Cidadão da União Europeia'*. We just knew it was called 'getting residency' and that if we were to be staying in Portugal for more than 183 days in a year then we needed it. We discovered that it was a temporary residency permit and would last for five years, and that after five years we could apply for permanent residency. We also knew that it used to be a nice glossy card to carry around but that now it is just a piece of A4 paper.

We decided to just walk in to the Câmara office in Lagoa and ask them what we needed to do. It would be the equivalent of visiting the town hall in the UK. We were sent into an open plan office and they all pointed to the young girl in the corner who spoke English and she sat us down and handed us a piece of paper which explained what paperwork she needed. We were off on the paper trail that was to begin our Portuguese Paperwork Folder ... or 'The File' as it was affectionately known!

For each of us we needed to have a photocopy of our passport (we showed our originals too) and a photocopy of our fiscal (tax identification) number on an official document. We have official fiscal cards, so that was easy. We needed to have a form called an *Atestado de Residência* (see below!) and documentation to prove our income.

Proof of income is basically to show that you can afford to live here in Portugal. I think you are supposed to show that you have at least the minimum wage coming in but as that is only about 650 euros a month for the Portuguese that's not much to prove. Bank statements, pension, investment interest, whatever you have that proves your income suffices.

The *Atestado de Residência* is where the fun begins! The young girl at the Câmara was very helpful, and she told us that we had to go to our local *Junta de Freguesia* or Parish Council office and that they would fill out a form for each of us. Then we had to take that form back to the Câmara with all our other photocopies and paperwork ... and fill in another form!

The Junta staff were very helpful too and they spoke a little English which was very useful. The *Atestado* is basically (another!) form that you get filled in and stamped by the Junta covering the area in which you live which proves your 'residency' i.e. where you live.

We needed to have photocopies of the same passport and fiscal number again, and a copy of our house deeds. We own our house, so we showed the paperwork we have that proves that we are registered at the Câmara as the owners. We only had a photocopy and that was fine. If you are renting, then you would show your rental agreement.

We decided to have an *Atestado* form each although the staff at the Junta offered to add me onto Dave's form as 'his wife' but we opted to do one each to be on the safe side.

The Junta gave us the forms to fill in and the list of papers we needed. We bundled all the paperwork together, went back to the Junta with our *Atestado* forms filled in (well half-filled in … we got a bit stuck so they helped us fill it out whilst we were there!) and we paid our fee which was only 5.10 euros each. That was on the Wednesday afternoon and the lady in the office said to us,

"Come back on Monday morning and your forms will be ready for you."

We did - and they were!

At this point, I have to say we were a little nervous, we had read Ben and Lou's book and they just seemed to have a nightmare getting all these forms and we seemed to be sailing through. We kept waiting for the problems to start ... but they never did!

We were on a roll, so we went straight from the Junta over to the Câmara office in Lagoa again clutching our folder full of forms and photocopies as required. We sat down, filled in the forms and signed them and then the young girl said to us,

"Now you must pay me."

We duly got our money out ... it was 15 euros each ...

"Oh no," she said, "you don't pay me here - you have to go out of the Câmara building, walk around the corner to the Finanças office and pay them. They will give you a form to say that you have paid me and then we can complete your paperwork."

We sat and worked out the layout of the building and the room we were currently sat in; and realised that if they had created a little 'serving hatch' through the wall we could have just sat there and handed over our money through the wall to the other side.

'Only in Portugal' we thought! So off we went, down the stairs, out of the main doors, around the corner, and into the next building, and the woman at the counter was waiting for us, printing off - yes, you've guessed it - more forms!! We paid, had our payment forms stamped, and then back we went around the corner to our nice young lady at the Câmara.

Then came the biggest surprise of all when she said to us,

"I have all I need, you can come back tomorrow morning and collect your *Residência* certificates, the 'mayor' will sign them this evening."

"Tomorrow morning - are you sure?!" we replied.

We were expecting to have to wait ages and we didn't have the heart to tell Ben and Louise that we had managed this all so painlessly!!

We went back the next morning and there they were sat on the desk waiting for us ... our shiny new *Residência* certificates, all signed and ready! Well they were not very shiny really as they were just on normal A4 paper. But it was a very nice feeling picking them up and going off for a coffee to celebrate ... although I must confess, I nearly spilt the coffee all over the folder with our new certificates in. I can't even imagine what the Câmara would have said if we had gone back half an hour later and said to them,

"You know those nice new certificates you gave us … can we have another set please?!"

Of course, that's just the beginning of it all as gaining residency triggered a whole new list of things we had to do. But we were legal, and we had the piece of paper each to prove it.

We were delighted to have secured this important document and happy to tell people that we were now resident. Local Portuguese friends were delighted and gave us the 'thumbs-up' sign; however, we had a rather less enthusiastic response from an English couple that we met at a gallery opening party a few days later. We walked over to them and they were talking to another couple about living in Portugal.

We said to them,

"Guess what, we've just gained our residency paperwork. We're all legal now!"

They looked at us in horror, wheeled around, stalked off and could be heard saying loudly to another group of people,

"You see that couple over there? They've just got residency here in Portugal."

They made the word 'residency' sound like a terrible illness we had contracted!

'Oh dear, two more friends to cross off the list then' I thought to myself.

---

1. Taylor, Louise and Ben. (2012). *Moving to Portugal: How a Young Couple Started a New Life in the Sun - and How You Could Do the Same.* Createspace Independent Pub.

14

Driving on the Right Side of the Law

Whilst chatting to friends Peter and Carol out here, we mentioned that we were looking for a small, economical Portuguese registered car. Peter said to us,

"What about that one over there?"

He pointed to a car parked in the back of his garage, which he was storing on behalf of a British friend who had left to go back to the UK to live. Five days later, and several thousand euros lighter in our bank account, we were the proud owners of a left-hand drive Portuguese car.

The price of cars out here is eye-wateringly expensive, due to a 'double-tax' rule that we don't really understand. It explains though why most Portuguese cars are leased or bought on a never-never-pay-it-off scheme. It's crazy, but it's just one of those things out here that you just have to shrug and accept as part of life. Having Peter around helped enormously at this stage, as it is highly recommended that you go to register your new car at the Institute of Registration and Notaries (or IRN) office with the previous owner, to ensure that they 'de-register' it and so that the office can check that no fines or outstanding finance is left on the car to be transferred over to you.

Out here you can end up holding more than a new set of car keys when you buy a car if you are not careful. It was our first introduction to Portuguese car bureaucracy and paperwork and as we already knew, the Portuguese do like paperwork! Thank goodness that we had Peter with us to explain everything and guide us through the maze of paper and separate offices and buildings that we needed to visit.

The one pleasant financial surprise was that our road tax was now only 35 euros a year. Car insurance is an interesting one, but comparative in price to the UK. We were recommended an English-speaking insurance company that cover the Iberian Peninsula, and they were very helpful. It's at times like that when you are sorting out car insurance, that we must admit, having your policy and all the paperwork written in English is just an extra reassurance. They also have insurance that is recognisably English; that is they offer fully comprehensive cover for any age of car as it is perfectly normal out here for Portuguese cars over 10 years old to only be given the option of having a simple third-party insurance. As cars tend to last quite well out here, probably because they don't have the British wet weather to rust them, this has always been a mystery to me. It's certainly cheaper to insure third party, that is until you have to pay up if something goes wrong. Perhaps it's just a British thing, wanting to be 'belt and braces' insured, but we were happy to find a company to insure us more fully.

The other thing to get used to is having to carry a small forest of paperwork with you in your vehicle wherever you are going. I ditched the small neat handbag I used to carry in the UK, trading up to a small overnight bag in order to carry everything I need out here ... and that was before we had a Portuguese car! Now we need an A4 folder full of more paperwork and copies of things than you would ever believe it was possible to carry.

It is almost a game when you are stopped by the Police (and yes, that happens frequently, for no reason at all other than 'we wanted to stop you' and it takes some getting used to). They will ask you if you have got x, y or z paperwork, and I reach over for the enormous folder stored in our car and start flicking through it. The police officer almost looks disappointed when you say yes and hand them the required papers.

One small tip for you ... even if you are resident and have the paperwork to prove it, the Police will always ask to see your passport. It's a pain to carry your original passport everywhere, but we discovered that you go to your local *Junta de Freguesia* (the equivalent of a local parish council office) and they will notarise a photocopy of your passport for you. If it has the official stamp, seal and signature from the Junta, that's enough for the Police to check, and means that you can leave your passport securely at home.

Driving on the 'other side' of the road has never been a problem for us; after the first hairy roundabout moment when you pick up the hire car from the airport, it has always been a natural thing. The same goes for sitting on the 'other side' of the car to drive; you might occasionally reach for the window handle on the way to the gear stick ... but it's not a problem. What was a problem however, and which rapidly turned into a very comical competition with some fierce scoring and whoops of glee every time one of us got it wrong, was the small matter of walking to the 'right' side (i.e. the left side) of the car if you were the driver. If we hadn't set up a very competitive and fiercely debated competition to 'keep score' we might have lost track of the number of times the driver went to the passenger side and vice versa. The highlight was when one of us (not saying which one!) got into the passenger side clutching the car keys and looked forward in complete bemusement at the lack of steering wheel in front of them!

✿ﺱﺲ✿ﺮ✿

Some of our friends have fared less well when it comes to having four wheels than us. Faced with the problem of having a UK registered car out here, and not being resident, they decided to matriculate their car. This meant filling in a mountain of paperwork, paying an extortionately large amount of import tax, and ending up with a very nice, but very expensively converted right-hand drive Portuguese plated and registered car.

They began the process in a somewhat innocent and hopeful state of expectancy. Four months later, they were left much wiser and slightly battered both financially and emotionally by the experience. It is not something that we would ever recommend to someone else unless they had a much-loved and treasured older vehicle that they couldn't bear to part with.

We offered to help them at the point where, having started the matriculation process, they got stuck in a maze of appointments and paperwork. It is not something you can start and then decide 'oh no, actually let's not bother' ... once those administrative wheels start rolling (excuse the pun!) they keep moving and you are caught up in a nightmare process of never-ending paperwork, costs and trips to various offices and buildings across the entire Algarve coast. Our friends had already found themselves trapped in a process of 'come back tomorrow and bring 'x' paperwork with you' so many times that they actually had to cancel a flight and re-book it for later that same week as one office they were dealing with refused to accept a UK bank card payment and they had to wait until they had wired over money to their Portuguese bank account and it had cleared before they could pay the import tax due.

They completed enough paperwork with their solicitor to allow us a 'power of attorney' position to take over the administrative reigns for them, and then the fun really began. We managed to get the car registered (or so we thought) at the IMTT office in Faro. We were given temporary paperwork to that effect anyway which should have been enough for us to then go to our local Finanças office and pay their road tax for them. They promised us that the proper registration document would be posted out shortly and that we could now go and pay the road tax.

The IMTT sent us off to another building ... of course ... to pay the road tax. Nothing is ever straight-forward here when it comes to anything that involves a piece of paper or some money. We knew the office they mentioned, as it is the IRN office where we registered the purchase of our own car when we bought it. We have always called it the 'cubby-hole' building as it is a tiny little office on a side street that seems to have people queueing out of the door every day clutching the ubiquitous little numbered ticket that keeps everything moving in Portugal at a snail's pace. Trust me you won't get anything done here without taking a ticket, shrugging at the others around you in a resigned fashion and then settling down for a long wait as you watch the numbers on the computer screen above you tick slowly forward until it is your turn.

I think we waited about an hour on this occasion, and after finally reaching the front of the queue, the man behind the desk took one look at the temporary paperwork I was clutching, shrugged at me, and turned me away, sending me off to another building to pay the road tax, whilst saying to me "not here, not here". Sadly, the amused expression he had fixed me with seemed to prove that he rather enjoyed knowing I had been queueing in the wrong place for all that time.

We duly trotted off to where he had told us to go, which was another Finanças building in another part of town, but this time we knew the man behind the counter and he is always really helpful, so we showed him the paperwork we had and explained that we wanted to pay the road tax on behalf of our friends. He said we could not pay it yet, and to return later, but every time we went to see him, he shrugged his shoulders, told us the car had not been registered on his computer yet, and to come back in another two weeks and try again.

The documents that we were expecting to arrive at our friend's address had also not arrived, despite the assurances from the IMTT office that they would only take two weeks to arrive, so we guessed that something was wrong. Eventually our nice friendly helpful man in the Finanças office made some phone calls for us, and it transpired that we should have taken the temporary paperwork we had to the man in the cubby hole that had turned us away, and he should have given us another form to complete to actually register the car.

To say we were confused … and fed up … by this stage would be an understatement. We thought the IMTT had registered the car, but apparently that wasn't the 'official' registration, it was just the 'initial' registration. Yes, you are now as confused as we were. Back to cubby-hole man we went, and after the usual ticket queueing, we got to his desk and he advised us,

"Oh yes you need to register the car here, you need to fill this form in. Who told you that you didn't need to do that?"

Oh well, actually … that was you. But it really wasn't worth trying to argue the point with him, so we tried to forge ahead and get things rectified. He handed us a form which required our friend's signature as the owner of the car. Cubby-hole man refused to accept a faxed or scanned copy of this, nor the 'power of attorney' paperwork that we had. No, it had to be two copies of the form, printed out, signed by hand, and delivered back to him. No problem … except that after all the weeks of going back and forth trying to get to this stage, we were exactly five days away from being fined for not registering the car with him … and knowing the postal system as well as we do, there was absolutely no way that was going to happen in time.

It took three weeks for the forms to come back to us in the post from the UK. A small matter of Christmas and the New Year got in the way of the pigeon and the small postal sack he was carrying, and we eventually returned to cubby-hole man on the 5th January when his little office re-opened.

We duly paid the fine and waited another three weeks for the paperwork to arrive. We then took that back to our nice man in Finanças armed with everything we could possibly find that related to the car in any way at all and asked to pay the road tax. Of course, by this time, we were also late paying that bill as well, so we expected to have to tell our friends that we were sorry, but they had to pay another fine. I think our nice man in there must have just felt sorry for us because … sssh don't tell anyone, we think this must be a record moment in Portuguese history … he waivered the fine for us.

It felt like a minor victory in an epic war. There seems to be something about matriculating a car over here that involves using the same administrative term in different offices to mean different things. We then had to find out if the car needed the equivalent of an MOT yet. In order to gain matriculation it had needed an MOT, which was duly completed, so it would have been easy to think 'ah that's ok, it's had an MOT, it must be ok now'. Oh no … that's a different MOT to the MOT that you need for a car every year or two years depending on how old the car is, that's just the matriculation MOT. It checks the same things as an MOT, looks like the paperwork that you get with an MOT pass ... but it's not an MOT. If you're not confused when you walk into one of these offices and select your ticket and take a seat ... you sure will be when you leave the office!

The moral of this story is quite easy though ... if you are thinking of matriculating your foreign vehicle in Portugal ... don't!

15

What's the Weather Like?

The latest headline in our local paper read 'Hottest May since records began' and in the last two years we have recorded the third hottest May June and September in continental Portugal since 1931, when records began. In September 2016 the average air temperature was set at just under 29 degrees Celsius over the entire month, and July 2018 saw the thermometer regularly hovering around the 38 degrees marker in the late afternoon.

"What's the weather like?" is usually the first question people ask us and the quickest way to annoy friends and family by replying,

"Oh it's 28 and sunny today," (almost ... every day!)

There is something quite magical about feeling the warm sun on your face and waking up to see the sun streaming through the shutters each morning. I know there are lots of research reports and studies into the health benefits of the sun; but it's at a far more basic level than that for me ... it just feels good! There is something deeply healing and soothing about walking along a beach in the sunshine or being able to sit outside eating fresh food and enjoying a chilled glass of wine as the sun sets.

There's also that wonderful poem people often quote about having time to stop and stare, and the hot sun out here certainly makes you want to slow down and enjoy the view. We have another dear old retired neighbour who lives near us who seems to spend hours just sitting on a deckchair outside his house, watching the world go by, and then at about 5 p.m. he goes for a walk around the local area, just seeing what has happened that day. He's been having a field day with us lately as we have been fixing our front fence. If only my Portuguese was up to following everything that he tells us, although I am starting to get the gist of some of it now though.

But I do think he's got it cracked, sitting there quite patiently enjoying the world around him; and giving out a few pointers on fencing every now and then. One of my aims from now on is going to be finding as many benches as I can to sit on for a while, and there are certainly plenty to choose from out here.

One other simple thing that I am enjoying is hanging out our washing in the sunshine. We lived in a flat with no garden for so long in the UK and now we have a proper rotary washing line outside. It is slightly more sophisticated though than some of the contraptions and lines we have seen strung up out here in Portugal. I am always amazed by the ingenuity of the locals who live on a fourth-floor apartment with a tiny balcony and yet have the most elaborate pulley system all rigged up for their washing that hangs out over their balcony onto the street below. It certainly doesn't take long for washing to dry out here in the summer, my record is seven wash loads all washed dried and put away in one day. Did someone mention ironed? No, that wasn't me … ironing at the best of times is a chore, but imagine doing it in 38 degrees' heat having a steam iron gushing out even more hot air at you? No thank you!

The peak summer months of July and August are quite a challenge at times; it must be said that the hot weather looks fabulous on a holiday forecast channel and can be brilliant for tourism. It can however also be blisteringly hot and strength-sapping too. We do not have air-conditioning, and for ten months of the year, that is fine, but there are some days when opening all the doors and windows and waiting for a cooling breeze to waft gently through the house just isn't enough. In fact, if there is a breeze, it is a breeze that is the equivalent of a hairdryer on full setting blazing straight back at you. You quickly shut the door and retreat inside whimpering.

No mention is made in the guidebooks of course of trying to live and work in the heat of summer. The house still needs its regular clean up, the shopping must still be collected, and tea cooked. We have perfected the art of having a nice salad in summer, presented alongside anything that can be cooked in ten minutes or less on the hob. The oven is made redundant, as the thought of turning on even more heat in the house is faintly ridiculous. We have often joked that the oven might be cooler than the kitchen anyway!

We think that the Portuguese people are constitutionally different to us, as we never fail to marvel at local people, especially youngsters, wearing tight jeans in the middle of summer, or wrapping themselves up against the harsh winter elements with so many knitted layers it is hard to see the person's face under the fluffy scarves. That is, of course, on the same day that we have decided that it is 'unseasonably warm' and have taken off our winter jumpers and have basked in the warm winter sunshine. We had a recent 'cooler spell' in July for a few days and the temperature dropped to a (rather pleasant) 28 degrees. Our Portuguese friends instantly started complaining about how cold it was and started reaching for their jumpers. Let's hope they don't have to ever visit the UK, where 28 degrees would virtually be the start of a heatwave in the summer.

There are of course gorgeous sunsets to enjoy every evening as well. We have the most amazing view from our kitchen window which looks right out over the Portimão river and straight at the setting sun. Somehow each evening in the summer as you watch the blazing sun set in the distance, you forgive it for frying you senseless all day and look forward to the sunrise again the next morning. Well I do anyway, as Kat the dog and I are out by 6.30 a.m. in the summer to enjoy our morning walk and be home again by 8 a.m. before the sun gets too hot. Yes it does get that hot that quickly out here in the summer, and I am especially careful of how hot the pavements get during the day when she is out for a walk.

It is a joke in our house that Dave has only ever managed to photograph one sunrise out here in all the years we have been here, and that was only because he had to take someone to the airport for an early morning flight. He is known for his beautiful sunsets and late evening shots rather than any sunrise spectaculars.

One shock we had though was finding out how cold a house can become the minute the sun disappears in the winter. Houses out here seem to be only designed for summer weather, they often have alarmingly large gaps around windows, especially at the top, and insulation is almost unheard of. Heating is usually via a wood burner, or pellet burner, but sadly we have neither, so we are forced to rely on electric heaters. We had a nice big one installed in the lounge, but we have an 'open plan' layout leading off from the front door and hallway, and open stairs both up to the bedrooms and down to the garage/studio area. It is not exactly conducive to keeping the heat in one room; although in the summer the same layout is wonderful for being able to open doors and windows and letting the breeze in.

We realised after our first winter here why so many shops sell lovely warm fluffy rugs and blankets in the supermarkets from about October onwards; they are less for decoration and more a requirement for huddling under in the evening.

Another shock was when it rains out here it really rains! We have had some torrential storms with pounding rain that certainly makes you think twice about popping outside. It does leave the car nice and clean though, and often the rain stops as suddenly as it began, and the afternoon is sunny and warm. We very rarely have rain that lasts for more than a few hours.

We had a surprise one morning, as I was down in the studio painting. A storm was forecast but the light was still good and there was no sign of rain on the horizon. I was busy at the easel when suddenly I heard what sounded like someone banging on the studio patio doors. Surprised I turned to look, not expecting to see anyone there. Our garden is secure, although we have been known to leave the drive gates unlocked, and the front garden gate is always unlocked. People rarely come around to the back of our house though, so I was not surprised to find no-one there when I looked around.

'That's odd' I thought but carried on painting.

Later that day we found out that a freak tornado had hit the Algarve, cutting a swathe across the region, and randomly decimating houses, cars and buildings. The tornado hit the shore around the Lagos town area and spread east, overturning cars, boats and structures almost randomly. We heard later that eight people were injured, mostly as they were sat in their cars that were overturned. A large roundabout at the entrance to Lagoa town showed the specific route taken by the tornado, as the roundabout has several large advertising hoardings along its route. Two hoardings had been ripped completely out of their foundations, and yet the hoardings either side were completely undamaged.

The church in Carvoeiro was struck by lightning resulting in a small fire, and the roof of Silves swimming pool was completely ripped off. The nearby football ground also suffered a lot of damage, and yet again, on either side of these structures everything was as normal. It was quite weird walking around there after the event and seeing the random damage that had been caused. We sat and worked out the timing of the tornado and it would have been passing where we live at the same time I had heard something pounding on the back door of the studio. I guess it was hoping to check in as it passed by. We looked again outside in the garden and there was absolutely no damage or sign of it having unleashed its power. I guess it is just one of those unexplained weather phenomena that happen.

❁ ❧ ❀ ❦ ❁

We were given slightly more warning of an impending storm linked to an unusual high tide one winter evening, Dave grabbed his camera, and we shot over to a local cliff area to watch the incoming storm. We were not alone; the road was strewn with cars and the cliff top was full of local people gathering almost in silence. The cliffs we were stood on were at least eighty foot above the sand below, so it was startling to suddenly see the waves crashing up alongside us. It was almost eerie to see the waves and storm striding towards us and churning up the sea. The local breakwater was submerged, and huge boulders were being tossed around like pebbles.

A powerful wave rode in and the local beach café was demolished in one hit. It smashed to pieces as if made of matchwood, the roof carried off in one piece into the sea. Food, stock, chairs, tables and random pieces of metal were carted off, scattered and tossed around, to a collective gasp from the audience above. It makes you realise how powerful nature really is when you witness something this dramatic in a local peaceful area that you know and love.

We have seen Ferragudo main square underwater several times over the years. If there is an exceptionally high tide, and the wrong weather conditions, the water comes swirling in, and nothing will stop it. The amusing thing is watching tourists still sat at the café tables, glass of beer or wine in hand, shorts on or trousers rolled up, whilst the staff gamely wade through the water to serve them, whilst simultaneously trying to sweep or mop out the water from their establishment.

April seems to be the worst month out here for rain, and the month is famous for its local sayings. One of the most popular is *'Abril, águas mil'* which translates roughly as 'April, a thousand waters' or 'April, a thousand rains.'

Of course, those are not the scenes we post on Facebook! We wait for a charming blue sky, preferably coinciding with dreadful stormy and rainy weather back in the UK, and then we post up how lovely and sunny it is here. Well, that's what social media is for, isn't it? Then we sit back and wait for the replies and comments to come flooding in (sorry, no pun intended!)

And no doubt as many British people do here, we shall continue to talk about the weather on a daily basis, especially through Facebook, and will also continue to annoy all our friends with our constant updates on how hot and sunny it is out here.

16

Random Acts of Portuguese Kindness

W e had to go to Faro recently to sort out some paperwork which involved us going to a Government building we had never heard of ... to get a piece of paper that was an official form that we had never heard of ... for a new law that had been passed that no-one had heard of ... you get the idea!

We checked the website of the building we needed, and it seemed to be easy to locate near the University, so I downloaded a map and off we went. We were soon hopelessly lost in Faro in a residential area somewhere off the map.

Armed with my little map and trusty basic Portuguese (well I could understand the words for go straight on, turn around, turn right, turn left and go around the roundabout ... they were usually enough!) I popped into a little café/coffee shop and asked for help. I love that about Portugal, you can walk into a new place that you have never visited before and the entire coffee shop occupants will come over to help you.

One older man was very helpful; he didn't speak much English but kept trying to work out how to get to the road we needed. We were so lost we weren't even on my map! He asked me where we were going and I told him the name of the building, then following more discussion across the bar between the man and the staff behind the counter, he picked up his coat and said,

"Follow me," and headed outside.

He then proceeded to drive his van halfway across Faro with us following, proudly stopping outside the necessary building and with a cheery wave of his hand he was off again. He didn't even stop to let us thank him properly, so we made a point of retracing our steps at the end of the day and leaving some money behind the counter at the café so that next time he went in he had a 'beer or two in the till'.

His gesture was so unexpected, and generous of him, but that was only the beginning of our help that day.

Once inside the said building we were greeted by a very friendly lady who came down from an office upstairs and who spoke some English for us. We got the gist of the fact that we needed to do something to a code on our financial paperwork, which required a trip somewhere else, but beyond that we had no idea what we had to do or where we had to go.

A young man who was also visiting the building and was sat the desk beside us came to our rescue. He explained exactly what we needed to do, and where we needed to go, and then asked us,

"Do you know where the Finanças office in Faro is?"

"No, sorry" came our reply.

"Oh, hang on a minute then, I'll finish up here and drive over there and you can follow me," he replied.

Another amazing act of kindness and an example of literally 'going out of your way' to help someone. We followed him all the way to the car park opposite the building we needed to visit, where he waved us goodbye and drove away.

So off we went to find the Finanças department and this is where we began to realise just how many hours are lost to bureaucracy and paperwork out here. Our first test was to go into the *Loja de Cidade* office, which is designed to be a one-stop-shop for citizens. They had the obligatory ticket machine displayed with a range of options to choose from. We had no idea which ticket we needed, so I walked up to the counter nearest to us to ask the lady behind the counter which ticket I required. I didn't even get chance to explain to her what I needed help with before she said to me,

"Green ticket."

I walked over to the machine and selected the green ticket option. The counter on the wall opposite said 'Green 27' so we waited. Thirty seconds later it snapped over to 'Green 28' which was our ticket, so, yes, you've guessed it, I walked back to the same lady at the same counter, showed her our green ticket and explained what we needed.

She promptly told us we were in the wrong place and that we wanted the Finanças offices which were hiding down another corridor ... and yes when we arrived there that involved another coloured ticket machine to select from!

This time we had to sit and wait our turn, watching the numbers slowly advance, all the time keeping an eye on the time, as they close for lunch at 12.30 p.m. and we arrived just before 12 noon. We made it with five minutes to spare which saved us having to return at 2 p.m. and resume queueing!

After a helpful spell there and some 're-coding', we had our updated financial paperwork ... but of course as it was now later than 12.30 p.m. the first building we went to was now shut for lunch until 2 p.m. so there was nothing else to do but wait. It was time for a long Portuguese lunch and some shopping.

And here was our next lovely surprise of the day. We went into a little side street café/snack bar which had a sign offering *prato do dia* (literally 'plate of the day') for 5 euros ... perfect we thought! We were greeted by the happiest chef we have ever seen. He was so proud of his food which was all laid out on view. He handed us a little spoonful of each of the main courses for us to try and his food was delicious. I chose the most wonderful *arroz de pato* (duck rice) and Dave had a very tasty piri-piri chicken.

It was quiet in the café and the chef came over after we had finished our meal and started chatting to us. We told him about the fun we were having with our paperwork and all the offices we had visited, and he commiserated with us and laughed about the Portuguese love of paperwork and systems. He wandered off and came back a couple of minutes later holding two large desserts, and handed them to us saying,

"For you, as a gift from me, to help you with the pain of your paperwork trail."

We were delighted with his kind gesture and tucked in.

After lunch we had time for a quick trip round a few local shops, then we went back to the first office we had started the day in ready for them to re-open at 2 p.m. All our paperwork was hopefully now in order and we could collect our special stamped piece of paper. Of course, that was not such a simple task, as the lady was called to the front counter from her upstairs office again. She came down after a few minutes clutching a piece of paper, which she showed us and asked us to check that everything was in order. We replied that it was and reached to take the paperwork from her off the desk in front of us.

"Oh no," she said, "not yet. First I have to stamp it to make it official."

She picked up the piece of paper, walked over to the stairs and climbed all the way back upstairs again, presumably to her office. We waited. About ten minutes later she returned brandishing the paperwork which now had an impressive embossed stamp in the corner.

"Now it is yours," she said, and handed us the all-important piece of paper.

We gratefully stuffed it into our folder, and then wandered over to the other side of the entrance area and had a look at their impressive collection of old petrol pumps. No, I don't know why they have them displayed there either! But they were rather fascinating if a little incongruous.

Then a first for us, we went to have a look round the Forum Algarve indoor shopping complex which had recently opened; and which is pretty much like every other 'shopping out of town' experience, although it did have some impressive fountains and water displays to enjoy too.

And then back to the car park to find our car. Multi-storey car parks out here have a fabulously complicated way of helping you to remember where you have parked. In the Forum car park if you can remember four things, namely a colour, a fruit, a letter and a number you'll be fine!

We have a rule here now which we have called 'one thing - one day'. The Portuguese do love their bureaucracy and paperwork and things here can take so long to sort out, so we have learnt to go with the flow now. We had spent all day in Faro, but we came away with the requisite new form that we needed, and we had some fantastic random acts of kindness along the way to reflect upon on our way back home.

17

Going Back to the UK for a Holiday

Sometimes it is only hindsight that gives you the view you need to decide that 'we'd do that differently next time'. Which is what we thought once we had completed our epic return trip to the UK for a holiday and made the simple and we though fun (!) decision to drive up through Spain and France and go through Le Tunnel.

We had talked to friends who had done the journey, and it didn't seem too far looking at the map, so we decided that it would be an adventure. It also meant that we didn't have to do the overnight ferry crossing again, which was something I was not actually in a hurry to repeat again anyway.

So now we have done it and it was one of those journeys (they always seem to happen to us!) that at least gave us plenty of new things to laugh about. And a list of top hints and tips to share with anyone else considering the same journey.

The first and most important thing is don't plan your route using the AA route planner and think you are calculating in miles and then gasp in horror when you work out how much petrol you need to travel '2,250 miles' ... not to mention how many hours it will take to drive that far. We had friends who said that it only took them 3 days to get to Northern France ... blimey we thought, that's a lot of driving overnight and driving over the national speed limit to cover that distance. Then I realised that I had been calculating the journey in kilometres not miles. Luckily 1,400 miles is a lot less mileage and a more manageable journey to contemplate.

Don't expect to drink a decent cup of coffee again once you leave Portugal. How I missed my lovely *uma bica* espresso for 70 cents a cup. As you travel north the coffee gets weaker and weaker and costs more and more money. In Spain it just tastes bitter and boring and in France we had two espressos delivered in paper specimen cups at a posh service station café and they charged us 3.40 euros for the privilege. And don't get me started on the soup bowl slosh that is called coffee in the UK!

Service stations are the same the world over, they charge extortionate amounts of money for over-cooked burger and chip menus. Salad? Healthy food? Forget it! The best or should that be the worst one was a service station in France called 'Mr Paul' where they wanted 4.20 euros for ONE macaroon biscuit!! And I will spare you the gory details of the various lovely service station toilets we used along the way.

But while I am on the subject of toilets ... (sorry!) ... where are all the toilet seats in France?! Somewhere in the rural interior of France there must be a farmer with a barn stacked full of toilet seats because I didn't see one in any of the public toilets.

We totally under-estimated the amount of driving to do on the first day. Let me assure you that almost two hours to the Portuguese border followed by a drive all the way up to the north of Spain ... in one day ... is quite a bit further than it looks on the map. Suffice to say our hotel check-in deadline was midnight and we arrived there at 11.55 p.m. We were met by a sweet girl on the reception who told us she had been worried about us all evening. The hotel when we finally arrived in Northern Spain was lovely, except the sink only had a hot tap ... who cleans their teeth with hot water?! It was bizarre! We were so shattered we crashed out quickly that night and morning seemed to arrive all too quickly.

Day two began our introduction to the wonderful tolls system. Spain isn't too bad; at least you can see where your money goes as we travelled through amazing tunnels carved out of the mountains as we curled our way into France.

And then there are the French tolls, and we found out that it is not cheap to travel through France and their extensive tolls system. Suffice to say that I have decided that France is just one giant toll booth, and you might just as well drive along with your window wound down, throwing 5 euro notes out of the window every 20 kilometres. That should just about cover it.

The worst thing about the tolls is the fact that you have no idea how much they are going to charge you. You roll up, stick out a hand and try to grab a ticket (the booths are craftily designed to be just out of reach most of the time ... and if you pull into a lorry one by mistake the machine is sixteen foot up in the air which is slightly 'awkward' !) and then you gleefully drive along a nice clean empty motorway thinking 'I wonder how much this one is going to cost us at the other end?' There are no signs telling you how much you will be charged or how far you can go before you reach another pay booth.

Half of the French motorways were being dug up and widened so at least we could see where our money was being spent, and this also ensured that we paid for the privilege of driving for miles along a restricted speed limit single lane route ... great! No chance of being caught speeding at least which we had been warned about.

And so to the second night of our stay and we had plumped for Le Mans on the map as it was halfway and seemed a sensible place to stop. Dave was in charge of booking the hotels on the way up and it was my turn on the way back, and we had a set budget of no more than 45 euros per night for accommodation, and we scored each other marks out of ten all the way. Oh yes, we are that competitive!!! Well what can I say about our second night's accommodation ... other than to tell you the name ... that should do it ... never book a hotel called Mr Bed (I kid you not!) and expect too much.

For those of you that have travelled on the Plymouth to Santander ferry you should be able to picture this one quite easily. They had recently refurbished the Pont Aven ferry when we travelled on it, and we now know where the old toilet/shower plastic pods went, as they are nestled into the rooms of the Mr Bed hotel, masquerading as 'en-suite' bathrooms.

Two small single beds, a sort of desk, the toilet pod and that was it. I think even a student backpacker would have been disappointed. They had 'child-proof' sockets for plugs too that were also 'plug-proof'. Oh dear, Dave was never going to score highly for this one.

But the best was yet to come the next morning when we went down to breakfast, for which they charged us 7.50 euros each. I naively wandered around looking for a plate to put my toast on (not too difficult to find you might think?) and the very kind and helpful young lad on duty said,

"Oh madam; we don't have any plates, you use a tray and put a napkin on top … that's your plate!" (Good grief!)

And so to Calais and more hotel fun! This one was not too bad except for its name; I do think the Trades Description Act should be enforced here for The Hotel Residence du Golf. I know, it sounds good doesn't it? I had lovely images of rolling countryside, green fairways, and lots of open space. I don't confess to know a thing about golf, but I do know that golf hotels are usually quite plush affairs. We arrived and looked around, it was not bad and if it wasn't misty, we could have seen the sea … but where was the golf? Oh, hang on a minute … I've found it! It was complete with a windmill, humps and little tunnels … yes … it was a crazy golf course situated next door.

Calais was only redeemed by one superb, inexpensive and wonderful restaurant called 'A Goût du Jour' which delivered simply one of the finest meals we had enjoyed in a long while, and they had tiramisu to die for! I know, that's so French.

And so to the tunnel … well not quite. My last piece of advice for this type of travelling is always leave plenty of time to reach the tunnel, even if your hotel is only five minutes away. That will give you time to empty the boot of the car (completely – and it was a bit full too!) and then change your tyre when you walk out in the morning and find that your tyre is completely flat.

We travelled nicely through Le Tunnel into the UK, although I can't recommend that the first sight of England you experience should be a service station on the M20 ... just don't do it! We almost hot-footed it back to Europe within 30 minutes of arriving in the UK.

We had a fabulous time visiting friends and seeing family, and quickly remembering why we moved abroad as the weather was shocking. We stayed with dear friends in Dorset and got very confused by the time difference (that makes it sound like we travelled across America doesn't it, rather than just up from France?!) Dave was a sweetie and got out of bed to make me a cup of tea at 7.20 a.m. one morning (lovely!) Except his watch was still on 'Spanish/French time, and it was only 6.20 a.m. (Not so lovely!).

And then it was time to complete the reverse journey back to Portugal.

18

Returning Home

We had a better experience at the Holiday Inn in Folkestone on the first night of our return journey; except why do they insist on charging extra for wi-fi? Even 'Mr Bed' didn't charge us for wi-fi (you will note that 'Mr Bed' has become the marker against which all other hotels are now judged, and with good reason).

Breakfast was a jolly affair. I am always slightly amused and scared in equal measure by the outdated toast-making contraptions that hotels seem to favour. The ones that look like a small medieval torture rack for toast, spinning round and plopping out burnt toast at the bottom. We had one at our Police training college and a badge of honour was handed out for all those of us that managed to set fire to the machine in the morning, to such an extent that a fire extinguisher was actually placed beside the machine.

It was the perfect moment for me to realise that I am looking forward to becoming old and slightly eccentric, as you can get away with anything when you are older. Picture the said toast torture chamber; a young man put his bread in and then walked away to wait for it to plop out at the other end. An old lady walked up, helped herself to his toast … and then when he returned for his toast and asked her if she had seen it, she innocently said to him,

"Oh sorry dear, they asked, and I said I didn't think it belonged to anyone so they [the waitress] took it away."

Ooooh! No they didn't – you cheeky thing! She tottered off clutching her plate of toast with not even the slightest trace of guilt on her face.

And then we were off to the tunnel and, of course, we managed to find ourselves in the 'this way please' lane leading up to the tunnel for their 'drugs and firearms' checks. At this point I should own up to something scandalous (!) One of the things that are very expensive to buy in Portugal are tea-bags (I know I know, how terribly British of me!) and it was one of the only things we stocked up on whilst we were in the UK. As the boot of the car was already a bit full (!) we emptied out all the boxes of tea bags we had bought and tucked all the little individual silver packs of tea bags into the corners of the boot. Add to that the fact that the entire back seat of our car was taken up by two enormous rolls of bubble wrap (being an artist requires a lot of strange items!!) and you can imagine my concern at being stopped and asked to 'empty the boot'.

The check involved rolling down the driver's window so the nice customs officer could check the steering wheel with what can only be described as a little duster on a pole. I was itching to ask him if he could wipe the whole dashboard as it was so dusty but a look from Dave silenced me! A quick check of the car (no emptying of the boot – phew!) and we were off again.

The tunnel itself was uneventful and very pleasant and the 35-minute journey really whizzed by. And then we were back onto the French motorway system again. It is a nice easy drive, and the brown tourist signs all along the roads had me faintly amused as they describe fascinating and intriguing chateaus and monuments at regular intervals; but I have to say that try as I might I couldn't actually see any of them. The signs didn't appear to relate to any upcoming junctions or exits on the motorway so I could not decide if they are just a decorative piece of tourist road enhancement or if they do actually relate to nearby buildings and attractions.

And so onto our second night's stay and after 'Mr Bed' I was quietly hoping for an easy victory in our hotel challenge. The picture on the website looked fine outlining the qualities of the Hotel Campanile near Poitiers. How could it possibly be worse than 'Mr Bed'?! Oh did I eat my words when we arrived at a faded and jaded 1970's style hi-de-hi holiday park. I had even paid more for a larger room with a double bed and an extra bed, so you cannot begin to imagine my disappointment to find ourselves given a key to a room that Harry Potter would have recognised as a replica of his cupboard under the stairs.

The extra bed turned out to be a small camp bed tucked under the double bed, and the room was so small I have no idea where or how you would have actually put the camp bed up if you had needed to use it! It was not quite how it looked online in their brochure.

Complaining proved fruitless to a member of staff whose only answer was,

"Sorry madam, maybe the picture you saw was from one of our other resorts."

I nearly choked with laughter at the thought of the place we were stuck with for the night being called a 'resort'. Oh well, perhaps dinner would be better. They were proudly advertising their high-quality restaurant on giant hoardings with what looked like steak and chips as the special on the menu for the night. Well, how can I put this? Have you ever had fresh steak before that came served formed perfectly into a beef burger shape complete with a cold pepper sauce?! No, me neither! As we both ordered the same luxury steak and they both came out looking like beef burgers, I can only assume that is what they think steak looks like.

After a hasty glance around the restaurant and spotting what looked like very average-looking breakfast cereals and pastries lined up ready for the following morning, we cancelled the breakfast buffet we had booked; which incidentally won the award for the most outrageous price of 9 euros each (!) and opted for a service station stop the next morning instead. Add that to a room that had one solitary tea bag between two people, and a square footage the size of a small cupboard and you can imagine how chuffed we were with staying there for the night. It did have one redeeming feature though … free wi-fi.

✧⁓✧◌✧

And so onto Spain and a trip through the amazing tunnels again and more tolls. We calculated that the return trip for some reason cost less than the way up and we had no idea why it was different as we had travelled exactly the same route.

Our next night was staying back at the Holiday Inn at Vitoria Gasteiz, which had proved to be an uneventful and comfortable stay on our way up and an easy choice on the way back ... or so we thought! Our room was hot when we arrived, and a quick fiddle with the air conditioning proved to have little effect, so we opened the windows, had a quick shower and went out for a walk. On our return the room was still oven-like, it had the gorgeous afternoon sun streaming through the window, and we realised that the air conditioning was not working. Added to that the shower head had a broken collar and drooped downwards at an interesting angle, so I decided to do the 'ask the receptionist for another room' phone call.

She came up to inspect our room and proceeded to have the most bizarre conversation with us, which went along the lines of me saying to her,

"The air conditioning is broken."

"Oh no, it is not broken, you can only have hot air in the winter, and cold air in the summer," she replied.

"Right, so it is the end of March and it's 23 degrees outside ... so is it summer or winter today?" I asked her.

"Oh it's winter so you cannot have it blowing cold air in here," came the reply.

She did let us change rooms to a room on the other side of the building ... and guess what ... the air conditioning didn't work in there either!

There is a small cotton socks postscript to this story too. Dave had rinsed out a pair of socks in the first room (guess who didn't pack enough clothes for the return journey?!) and he left them hanging out of the window to dry ... so our apologies to the cleaner who would have arrived in our first room and found it all empty and immaculate ... except for the strange pair of socks dangling from the window!!

The Holiday Inn did get extra brownie points for a lovely breakfast which was included in the room price. As typically British travellers we turned up in jeans and T-shirts for the buffet breakfast and felt woefully inadequate next to the perfectly made up and beautifully dressed women (and smartly dressed men!) with their well-behaved and immaculately dressed children.

I do have a question about Spain though, which is why do the Spanish appear to be obsessed with fried eggs?! We went to a very nice little bistro restaurant and ordered fish of the day and the plate came out with a nice piece of grilled fish, with some fried squid rings, chips and salad .... and a fried egg. Weird!

Even stranger than that though is the Spanish *tortilla*. Although it translates as an omelette, it has various fillings on offer, usually ham or chorizo. We were not expecting the omelette to come out from the kitchen folded up and wrapped in a baguette though.

Food prize of the trip must go to a very nice little restaurant we found in Salamanca, with a small warning that most restaurants don't seem to even start serving food until 8 p.m. in Spain. The menu was solely in Spanish (it is so different to Portuguese, and we are quite fluent around a Portuguese menu now) so it was a shock for us to not recognise hardly anything on offer. We decided to bravely plump for things without having a clue what they were, although I cheated a bit for my main course as I knew what *pollo* was … you can't go too wrong with chicken, can you?! The starters turned out fine, but Dave's main course was hilarious. The plate came out containing two large meat covered balls and a stringy piece of something … well I'm still not certain what it was ... but I know what it looked like! So even if it wasn't ... (why let the truth stand in the way of a good story?!) we told friends that he had eaten bull's testicles for dinner. With a fried egg of course!

Salamanca was beautiful, it is such an amazingly historic and delightful place and it was well worth the extra night's stop-over to be able to have time to wander the streets and soak up the sights. Dave took some lovely shots, although a small word of warning …

do your homework before you set up your camera. The Plaza Mayor in Salamanca is an exceptionally beautiful place; and reminded me instantly of St Mark's Square in Venice. It has stunning architecture, a wide-open square absolutely bustling with people, with students sat all over the floor, hen parties (!) and cafés with liveried waiters. It is a stunning architectural feast for the eyes and the camera lens. It is at its absolute best at night, lit up and twinkling ... well it was until about five minutes after Dave started setting up his camera, when all the lights went out! We forgot to research that one ... trust us to try to take shots on Earth Day, which is the day every major monument across the world goes dark for an hour.

Salamanca is also the venue for my famous hotel victory over Dave. We were a bit 'neck and neck' to this point scoring each other's hotel bookings, and it all hinged on the Hotel Regio I had booked for our last night. I was quietly confident as it was a 179 euros room (with breakfast included) discounted down to 45 euros for the night. I knew I had won the minute we walked into the faded art deco grandeur of an amazing reception and hallway and I danced a jig when we saw the room we had been given for the night; it was beautiful. I won hands down! It was a big room, with a huge TV, free wi-fi, a lovely big bathroom (with big fluffy towels!) and we even had a balcony. And did I mention the sumptuous (free!) breakfast ... and the fact there was a bus service that stopped right outside the hotel that took us into the centre of Salamanca. The reception staff even gave us a map and circled the main sights for us. Result!

It's also worth finding out when the bank holidays occur in different countries as we fancied a quick stop-over at Ikea in Seville. We had planned on having their meatballs for tea followed by a quick wander round the store as we can always find something to buy in Ikea. We arrived outside the store and were amazed to find it was closed, as Ikea is always open. But not on April 1st we discovered, as it is a Spanish holiday.

So we gave up our plans for a sneaky shopping trip which was probably for the best as I have no idea where we would have put anything we purchased in our already laden car, and we carried on to the final border with the lovely 'Welcome to Portugal' sign which signalled we were home.

I am not sure we will be in a hurry to do the same route again, although it has given us a taste for travelling. There is so much of central and northern Portugal that we are longing to see. Next time we will make sure we research the hotels more closely and check out all the national holidays in advance though.

19

The X-rated Expats

We have met so many truly fantastic and special expats living out here, many of whom have lived here for many years, have a full and busy social life, or work hard and run their own business. Many speak fluent Portuguese, and they are always full of interesting stories when you meet them. Maybe that's just the type of people that we are drawn to.

We have also met our fair share of X-rated expats too, most of whom seem to fit quite neatly into one or more of the following 'tongue-in-cheek' categories:

'The Socialite'

This person thrives on being the centre of attention and will always be sat in a posh restaurant surrounded by their friends. They will greet you like a long-lost best friend with a loud,

"Oh dah-ling, how lovely to see you, we must get together soon."

Which roughly translates as 'look at me, I have so many friends, I know everyone', and which will be accompanied by lots of 'mwah mwah' noises and air-kissing.

You won't see them again for at least six months, and they will go through the same ritual again the next time that they see you.

'The Drinker'

The Algarve does seem to have more than its fair share of expat drinkers. You can usually spot them ordering a large beer at a beach-side café at about 10 in the morning or drinking several litre carafes of cheap wine at lunchtime. They will move on to another café in the sunshine in the afternoon for more 'drinkies' and sadly some of them then consider driving home afterwards.

'The Swinger'

There are so many golf courses on the Algarve that you are bound to bump into a golfing expat or three out here, which is fine if you are a fellow golfer and can understand all of the golf chatter, otherwise you will quickly find your attention wandering and start amusing yourself by making up stories in your head about who would combine those lemon yellow trousers with that diamond patterned multi-coloured jumper.

And talking of wandering ... sadly that's not the only kind of 'swinging' here on the Algarve. Apparently, there is a thriving 'swinging set' out here too, although thankfully we have never been invited to try that 'sport'.

'The non-resident Resident'

This expat will have lived here on the Algarve for many years, full-time apart from the occasional trip back home, usually to the UK (see the UK Car Driver category below) and they will very proudly inform you that they haven't taken out residency and have no intention of ever doing so. If they are ever stop-checked or asked for their documents, they state that are 'on holiday' and are scornful of ever being legal in the country they are living in.

Interestingly these are often the same people who are loudly vocal about the 'illegal immigrants' in the UK who are 'scrounging off the welfare state' and who should be 'deported'. This is usually fuelled by the latest UK newspaper that they have sat beside their large beer at the local café and is said loudly enough so that everyone around them can hear them.

'The UK Car Driver'

If you looked carefully at many of the UK plated cars out here before the law on displaying tax discs changed, you would probably have found that the tax disc ran out a couple of years ago, and just like the non-resident Resident above, if they were stopped by the police, they would say they were 'just on holiday'. They will probably drive their car back to the UK each year for its MOT, although up until a few years ago you could even buy an MOT from a guy in a pub here on the Algarve. Well that was until he was arrested and charged with multiple fraud offences.

They will also probably have declared their car as SORN (off-road) in the UK if their tax is out of date, and naively think that their insurance will cover them if they have an accident.

'The Ex-con Expat'

You are bound to run into a shady character or two in a bar somewhere out here. We met one man who very proudly told us that when he and his wife moved out here to live, they went to their local furniture showroom in the UK and ordered a whole new set of furniture on their 'buy now – pay later – with nothing to pay for twelve months' scheme. They then had it all shipped out here just before leaving their UK address, and have never paid a penny for the furniture since. Presumably they have never been able to set foot in the UK again either. And that was his serious recommendation to us as to how we should furnish our property out here when we met them.

Sadly for him the conversation took a distinct turn for the worse, when, after finishing telling us all this, he turned to Dave and said,

"So, Dave, what do you do for a living then?"

Dave replied: "I'm a police officer."

It's funny but we never saw him again.

'The Expat Moaner'

There is one in every bar and online forum, the person who just has to moan about living out here. There will always be something that they don't like, which can range from the GNR police, the fines, the taxes, the food, the Portuguese people, the language barrier, the fact that kit-kats are so expensive out here, the hot weather … it's too hot; the cold winters … it's too cold, the price of a daily British newspaper. You name it, they'll moan about it.

It does make you wonder why they are living here at all.

'The UK Food Shopper'

Often closely related to the Moaner, is the expat that insists on having Crunchy Nut Cornflakes, Robertson's marmalade and Andrex toilet paper. Admittedly they are probably a lot happier now that Iceland has opened two stores here on the Algarve, but the number of green plastic delivery crates from Asda which arrive here from the UK with alarmingly regularity via a shipping company, will attest to the number of expats who still shop in the UK and have all of their food delivered over here. These are the same people who proudly tell you that they wouldn't dream of eating any 'foreign muck' out here.

Luckily there are so many bars out here that will serve a full English breakfast, steak pie and chips or other English food that they probably never need to worry!

'The Jet-set Expat'

With their 'little boat' (for that, read 'giant yacht moored in the harbour') and their casual 'come round for drinkies and nibbles next Friday' (for that, read 'garden party for 200 guests with an outside catering firm and a marquee in the garden') these expats inhabit a different world to the rest of us. They are always popping back to the UK on a chartered flight to go to a party in London for the weekend, then travelling back to the Algarve to lie in the sun beside their custom-built swimming pool, before heading out to another posh restaurant for dinner. The kitchen in their luxury villa is still brand new and has probably never been used.

They inhabit a world of luxury cars, champagne, and red-carpet parties usually found only in a glossy magazine.

'The Dodgy Dealer'

'Non-resident' for tax purposes … of course … this person will have set up numerous businesses over the years, mostly to do with cars, or catering, or providing a full UK TV download service, or offering interesting financial investment opportunities. Each time that you see them, they will invite you to their next 'grand opening-night party' and hand you a new shiny business card. Twelve months later, when you see them again, they will have moved on to the 'next big thing' and will hand you another business card!

'The Winter Caravanner'

Not strictly an expat but amusing nonetheless; are the caravan crowd that descend on the area about October each year. They usually coincide with the end of the main mosquito season, and almost overnight it is as if they have all been given the same sign; like migrating birds moving to a warmer climate, a swarm of caravans will descend on a car park or patch of wasteland, pick their spot and settle in for the winter. Many of them have elaborate satellite systems installed to ensure that they don't miss any of their weekly soap operas.

Once they have finished erecting their elaborate awnings and fairy lights, they will proceed to bring out the items of furniture that must come as standard with all caravans, namely the two deck chairs and small square folding table that appear to be an obligatory part of the caravan experience. It is hilarious on a lovely afternoon to walk past row after row of caravans parked up. The town of Silves has a municipal car park that has swarms of caravans every winter and almost every single one of them will have the two deck chairs and table outside all facing in the same direction, often with the cheery occupants sat perched in them reading a book or the daily newspaper.

At least once every winter however the caravanners are less than cheerful when the local police descend and fine each one of them for parking illegally. Silves council has a fierce reputation for this, and each time the ensuing melee in the local press makes for an interesting read: should they be parked there, do they contribute to the local economy, should the police act in the way that they do. It's all gripping stuff, but I'm always far more interested to find out if they are fined more for having the matching deck chairs and table plonked outside their pitch.

'The Eco-Expat'

These guys are usually not really 'X-rated' but there are an interesting and growing band of eco-warriors living here that have a fascinating range of yurt tents, free-range chickens and solar panels that ensure they are carving out a small, but significant to them, eco-footprint. We have met people that live completely off-grid; ones that run eco-friendly holidays, ones that travel only by bike or walk, and ones that are self-sufficient in terms of food and heating.

The Algarve seems to cater well for them, and similarly doesn't seem too bothered by them. There are so many off the beaten track farms and stretches of land that have interesting dwellings attached to them, with occupants that live simply and quietly alongside their Portuguese counterparts, trading food and crafts, and living a life not dissimilar to how many local people live anyway.

'The Brexit Expat'

We have met British people who live out here who proudly tell us that they voted for Brexit. Without entering the political arena too deeply, it always amazes me that they can happily live in Portugal as a welcomed and well-looked after immigrant; and yet if you ask them why they voted to leave, they almost always mention that there are 'too many immigrants in Britain'. The irony is not lost on me.

I have likened it to the turkey that votes for Christmas, goes out to the local supermarket and buys the potatoes, brussels sprouts and other vegetables, comes home, prepares the meal, switches on the oven and sits in the kitchen waiting …

20

Food and Drink

One of the things that we like about living here is the simple way of life and diet that we now have. Gone are the days of getting home from work in the UK at 8.30 p.m. and dashing round to the local pub to order some food before they stopped serving at 9 p.m. Long summer evenings are spent sat outside, savouring the fresh food, beautiful warm weather and spending real time together, talking, laughing, and enjoying the company of friends and a fine view. And that's just when we are at home! We really enjoy finding local restaurants, where we can enjoy simple traditional food, surrounded by Portuguese people, and where we can still get change from 30 euros for a meal for two.

Prato do dia (which literally translates as 'plate of the day') is very common out here, especially at lunchtime, and if you know where to go, you can have a three-course meal, with a drink and a coffee afterwards for 8.50 euros each. Often there is a choice of three or four main dishes to choose from, usually a couple of meat dishes, fish and sometimes a vegetarian option. Being a vegetarian out here is a little more difficult though, in a small restaurant there is often a limited choice for non-meat eaters, as meat and fish rule the menus here.

If meat is your thing though then you are spoilt for choice. Chicken, pork and beef are all common meats, but you can also enjoy a fine rabbit stew, or a Brazilian thin steak called *picanha*; or *porco preto*, which is pork from the Iberian black pig, or even one of the local delicacies ... wild boar.

But one of the finest things to try out here must be fish. If you are lucky, and like fresh fish, and can find a person 'in the know' then you can ask for directions to an all-you-can-eat local fish restaurant. One of our favourites is called 'Zé Leiteiro' in Armação de Pêra which is known to all the locals. They have just a few tables and benches outside and more spaces inside, and you sit beside your fellow diners and enjoy plate after plate of the most amazing array of different fish and seafood ... all for only 13.50 euros per head. If you don't manage to eat at least eight different platefuls of fish, the waiting staff look disappointed! We've enjoyed plate after plate of robalo, sea bass, salmon, squid, mackerel and sardines until we could literally eat no more.

Other end of the scale (excuse the pun!) are the restaurants that serve fish 'by the kilo' on the menu. They will bring you over a delightful looking whole fish and you will have no idea how much the thing is going to cost you until the bill arrives. You can be sure though that you have paid for every bone too!

Fish aficionados will love visiting the local market and seeing the display of shiny locally caught fish lined up ready to buy. There are so many names, colours, shapes and sizes to choose from. Sadly I now know the names of many of them in Portuguese but have no idea what the English equivalent would be, so when friends come to stay they just have to trust me that the 'pinkie one with the bright shiny eyes over there on the counter' is really nice!

One of the other delights out here are the oranges which are grown and sold in abundance. Driving past orange groves in the countryside is such a treat, whether that is to enjoy the heady scent of the blossom, or watching the fruit ripen in the sunshine. You can buy them at the side of the road almost anywhere; however we have our favourite old farmer that we visit in a nearby tiny village. It's not just that his oranges are so sweet and juicy; it's the whole experience of buying them from him that we enjoy.

Long retired but obviously happy to bolster up his meagre state pension, he still tends to his trees even though he is well in his eighties. His genuine pride in his fruit is a delight, his stall is set up in his front garden, and the wonderful old set of scales he uses to weigh up the fruit with could well have come from the 19th century. Why he uses the scales is a mystery though, as you ask him for a kilo of oranges, then you select the ones from the crates that you want, he puts them in a carrier bag, weighs them meticulously, tells you it will cost 1.50 euros … then promptly proceeds to grab at least another four oranges and a handful of satsumas and adds them to bag.

He then carefully selects two more oranges, wipes them gently with his fingers, and hands them to you. The first time he did this I made the equivalent of a major countryside social faux pas by thanking him, adding them to the already bulging bag of fruit and walking off smiling and waving to him. The next time he patiently showed us that the special extra fruit selected by him are for eating there and then, as he proceeded to peel them and hand us the fruit. It is the rural equivalent out here of 'try before you buy' and is quite a ritual. Sometimes we stand there trying the oranges, the satsumas and the clementines for him, all the time trying to make polite conversation in pidgin Portuguese. We knew we had 'made it' the time he called his wife over to join us and solemnly introduced us to her as his 'foreign friends'. We now call him 'Senhor Laranja' (Mr Orange) and are disappointed if we drive through the village and cannot stop to see him and buy some fruit.

Although the local major supermarkets all stock a wide range of fruit and vegetables, the local markets are more traditional, and it is fun to see what fruit and veg are in season and to buy things as they appear. Compared with the UK, less fruit and vegetables are shipped in from overseas, although sadly that does seem to be changing. There is something exciting about realising that it is now 'fig time' and to see crates of fresh figs arrive in the market each summer. A dollop of honey and some Greek yoghurt and those figs taste amazing. Our neighbour is much more organised and domesticated than us, as some of her figs will be carefully dried and made into a delicious fig jam ready for Christmas. I always look at our empty crate, lined with fig leaves after we have scoffed them all, and think 'maybe next year we'll make jam' … but who am I kidding? That's never going to happen!

Another delight we have discovered out here is tomato jam. In the UK if you had handed me toast covered in tomato jam, I would have laughed at you. Maybe it is the sunshine out here that makes it sound, and taste, just fine. Finding marmalade out here on the other hand, was quite a challenge. Long before the day that the Overseas Iceland supermarket arrived out here and made it possible to buy, at a price, quite a lot of British products; marmalade was always the food that I missed. Proper marmalade, with chunks of peel and fruit in it. The stuff that you put on your toast in the morning with a mug of tea. You can take the girl out of Birmingham ... but …

You would think with this surfeit of oranges and lemons growing out here that marmalade would be easy to find. The Portuguese sell a product out here that translates as marmalade, which comes in a margarine type tub. Do not be fooled, it has the consistency and flavour of a peach jam. It certainly does not scream out 'eat me eat me, put me on your toast in the morning'. It became a personal quest to find 'the real thing' and luckily Aldi the German supermarket eventually came to the rescue. They now sell a fabulous little range of orange and lemon jams that the British would call marmalade and finally peace and contentment has been restored to my breakfast time each day.

✿ﻬ✿ଓ✿

It is amazing that it is almost always the small things that make a difference. If you were to ask most British people out here what culinary contraband makes its way into their suitcases when they are holidaying, or living out here, and I can guarantee most of them will mention tea bags. It's such a British thing isn't it, putting the kettle on to make a cuppa. It is one of the few things I will visit the Iceland store for, to stock up on tea bags in their hundreds. (The packets that came back as 'contraband' in the boot of our car from our trip back to the UK did not last very long!)

Apart from that, we are very Portuguese in our drinking habits, and have grown to love the local espresso style *bica* of coffee that arrives in a tiny cup with an even tinier spoon and obligatory sachet of sugar. We will usually omit to order the local accompanying brandy at 9 a.m. but ordering a *bica* in a local café is almost a daily ritual now. If they know us in a local café then we are fine, but if we go anywhere else it can be quite amusing. We go in, say *"bom dia"* (regardless of the time of day!) and ask for *"duas bicas faz favor"* (two coffees please). Often the server will reply *"duas bicas?"* with a question and we reply *"sim"* (yes). Sometimes we go around this question and answer two or three times, even being asked *"um café?"* (another word for the same thing) with a distinct questioning 'are you sure?!' tone to the words. Once we even had a waiter go and get an espresso cup and bring it over and wave it at us saying in English,

"Are you sure, you want one of these?"

We cannot be the only British people in Portugal that like their coffee the same way as the Portuguese? And yet so often we are asked at least twice to check that we are ordering the right thing. I guess that a lot of British people order 'coffee with milk' so they assume that's what we want. But we love the sweet strong tiny little coffee that packs a punch. Of course it also goes extremely well with a little *pastel de nata* on the side, a lovely indulgent little cake which is a bit like an egg custard tart, sprinkled on top with cinnamon, and if you are lucky, still warm from the oven. It's no wonder whole mornings just seem to disappear out here, as you sit in the sunshine at a little café in the square, with a coffee and a cake, watching the world, and the tourists, go by.

Another food that is very common here is the local favourite of piri-piri chicken, which is always accompanied by chips and a side salad and is washed down rather nicely with a beer or two. The town of Guia will tell you that their region is the true home of piri-piri chicken, and at the end of the Guia shopping area on the N125 road, the roundabout with its giant ornamental gaudy chickens sat proudly on the middle of the roundabout will help to remind you.

You have to watch some of the menus out here though, we have been caught out loads of times by a menu that seems very reasonable, say 8.50 euros for piri-piri chicken, and then when the bill arrives for two people it's nearly 30 euros. It's the *couvert* or starters that can really add to the bill, that tempting basket of bread, butter, sardine pâté and little bowl of garlic carrots. Some restaurants add up every single one of those items individually, and you don't really notice the prices until the bill arrives. Move away from the tourist areas though and you will often be charged only 2 or 3 euros each for the whole couvert package, that's if you decide to select it at all. We often decline it when it arrives, waiters aren't offended, and you don't have to have it.

The best piri-piri chicken and where to go is a difficult decision. If we are near Guia we turn off at 'chicken roundabout' and head to the village of Algoz, as it is less than ten minutes away, but they have two of the best restaurants for piri-piri chicken. One is huge, like a big car showroom full of tables, with a queue in the summer that will reach into the car park outside as people patiently wait hours for a table to become free. The other is smaller, with a cosier feel and an abundance of stuffed and colourful chicken toys to entertain children of all ages! The warehouse one is called O'Marinhos and the smaller one is O'Martinhos ... yes, it's easy to get confused! The business owners of the large one started off in the smaller one then outgrew it and moved round the corner; and the owners of the smaller property then thought they would take on the challenge of creating the finest piri-piri chicken in the Algarve! It's a fiercely contested thing.

The tradition with piri-piri chicken is apparently to have a scrawny little bird with tiny wings served up on your platter; however personally we're not really convinced and if we get the chance we head up to Fóia above Monchique in time for sunset and order piri-piri chicken at one of the local restaurants on the hill.

Pick an outside table and the view is stupendous. What is truly amazing though is their local piri-piri chicken, which is an enormous platter of fat juicy chicken pieces sat guzzling up the oil and juices below, with fabulous home-made chips and a nice big salad. And you will have change from 30 euros for two, unless you are led astray by an awesome fridge full of cakes! My top tip for dessert is always go for the *doce de casa* (literal translation 'pudding of the house') if you are not sure what to order. It will differ wherever you go, but will usually involve a combination of cream, biscuits and a custard-like cold bit in the middle that sounds rather average but always delights.

One thing that we cannot personally recommend, although it's probably worth trying once just to say that you have tried it, is the local alcoholic shot called Medronho. It's made from the berries of the Medronho tree, or strawberry tree, and is an innocuous looking clear liquid that the waiter may well offer you 'on the house' at the end of the meal. It's the expression on their face that you need to watch out for, that should tell you all that you need to know. If you're in the Monchique area they will always bring it out at the end of the meal for you to sample. It's the knowing, sage-like expression of the waiter that says: 'I'm very proud of this, go on, I dare you to try it' that should warn you off. Let's just say if you want to sprout a few new hairs on your chest then go for it! And if you are ever in a Portuguese restaurant until late one evening watching Liverpool win the European Cup after extra time and penalties; and the owners stay open specially for you to watch the end of the football … and then the father comes over and says,

"Now you must try my home-made Medronho" … well all I can say is, you probably won't remember the walk home to your house afterwards!

The Portuguese like their spices and herbs, and a visit to any of the fairs and markets, or especially the medieval fairs in the summer, will introduce you to a vast array of colourful herbs and powders to delight your senses and enhance the kitchen selection. We did however draw the line at the collection of herbs on display at a fairground event last summer though; with names like 'Enlarger' and 'Gout Cure' on offer we politely declined and moved on to the *fatura* stall!

Not to be confused with the name of the receipts (*facturas*) that you get out here; a *fatura* is an outrageously nice deep-fried battered delight that tastes a bit like a doughnut, which is dipped in cinnamon and sugar and looks faintly rude. It's one thing that I can't resist in the summer months, that and a rather lovely and equally unhealthy *doce de leite* (sweet milk) flavoured local ice-cream. It's a good job we do a lot of walking to balance these things out.

The longer we live here, the more we have come to appreciate the simple yet hearty food on offer. Rabbit stew with a juice that soaks up into the bread sat at the bottom of the bowl; *salada de polvo* (octopus salad) with a side order of calamari rings; *picanha* steak with a generous helping of grilled pineapple rings on top, home-made chips; cataplanas with fish and mussels; mackerel or sardines inside a hunk of bread; and a nice chilled *vinho verde* green wine, and my favourite dessert name of all time which is called *baba de camelo*.

When we first ordered this, I thought I had discovered the best dessert ever invented. Think condensed milk, boiled until it turns to caramel and left to cool. Quite frankly the bowl can never be big enough. I had thought for ages that the dessert was called *baba de caramelo*. I had no idea what a *baba* was, but we knew it referred to the caramel pudding. Then I discovered to our great amusement one evening that *baba* means 'spit' or 'dribble' and that the second word is actually *camelo*. Which translates nicely as 'camel spit'.

No … it didn't put me off for a second!

21

Things That I Have Learnt

Looking back now there are some things that are obvious to us now that I wish I had known about from the start. Life here is simpler, less stressful and less complicated. Things work out at a different, slower pace. And you need far less than you imagine you will need. So here are some things that I wish someone had told me before we moved out here to live:

You really will wear shorts and T-shirts every day in the spring, summer and autumn. You will not wear at least 80% of the wardrobe of clothes that you brought out from the UK, and you won't need all those posh tops and skirts that you packed 'just in case'. Casual means just that out here. Even if you go to a posh event, the dress code will still be quite casual. It is too warm here for most of the year to wear anything other than simple attire. Cotton and linen clothes are excellent, polyester and thick man-made fibres are not so great.

You will live in sandals, flip-flops or 'slaps' for around eight months of the year so make sure they are good ones!

You will need some warm jumpers, fleeces and jeans in the winter. But probably not that fur-lined full-length winter coat. Or those posh leather knee-high boots and long skirts.

In the winter months you will revert to your 70's childhood with a sudden desire for warm layers; you will crave warming soups and stews; and fleecy blankets and hot water bottles. Be warned that it does get cold in the evenings and at night out here.

You can buy most toiletries out here the same as in the UK, but they are often more expensive. And there aren't any big department stores with rows of make-up counters and millions of products and designer ranges to choose from. 'Going natural' when it comes to wearing make-up is definitely easier when for most of the year you can catch some sun and have a nice natural glow to your face ... well unless like me of course you burn easily and need to wear some sunscreen even in the winter.

✧ɬ✧ɣ✧

You won't keep in touch with all the people that promise to keep in touch with you when you leave. Probably only about a third of them. That's just life, but you will be pleasantly surprised by how easily and well you stay in touch with some people. Skype and Facebook are great for that and have made communication effortless and immediate.

You will miss family and some friends a lot. But you'll miss them at odd times when you least expect it and often right after you have just called them on Skype. But the holiday times when you get together and/or travel back to the UK to spend time with them and see them will be special.

When friends come to stay with you, it will cost you extra. Even if they kindly offer to give you some money to cover their stay. You will stock up the fridge with extra food, eat out more often whilst they are staying with you, and if you are like us, you will of course insist on paying your fair share. And there are only so many times you want to visit a major theme park or attraction, so it is perfectly fine to tell them to have a nice time and you will see them later when they return. And as much as you like your friends, you will probably sink into the nearest armchair when they have gone out; and have a quick nap!

Life in the sun is just that ... it's life and there's a lot more sun!

But there is still the shopping and laundry to do and the bathroom to clean. You still have routines and jobs to do but you just might go a bit slower in the hottest part of the day or put things off until the evening ... or the autumn!

You can hang your washing out on the line in the morning and it will be dry the same day or within an hour in the summer months.

And when the sun is shining and you've got work to do … even if that work involves the joyous fun of putting paint onto a canvas, you will still look enviously out of the window at the gorgeous sunshine and blue skies. You're just more likely to play hooky!

You will find yourself slowing down and enjoying life so much more easily. Going for a stroll in the afternoon sun, catching an extra ten minutes sat in the sun outside, and long leisurely lunches will become the norm.

You will never be hurried to pay your bill in a restaurant, and you will be expected to slowly enjoy your final drink or coffee.

❖❧❖❧❖

Learning the language is a must. Not so much for important tasks as we have yet to find a shop/bank/agency that doesn't have an English speaking assistant if you are stuck; but much more importantly for you to build friendships and meaningful relationships with local people and to know what is happening around you.

You will find an English – Portuguese translation app on your phone indispensable.

There are lots of different types of expats and you will learn to find your own friends. Just because you both speak the same language doesn't necessarily mean that you will have much in common. But you can also meet new and fascinating people from all nationalities and backgrounds. The Algarve tends to 'flatten out' people socially, and unless you are frequenting what is locally known as the 'Golden Triangle' area, where every other car is a Jaguar and the handbags and jewellery are all 'fabulously expensive darling'; you can find genuine and honestly nice people from all walks of life sat down enjoying a coffee or a beer together.

You will drink more coffee! And if you're not careful, drink more beer and wine than you ever would in the UK.

You will greet total strangers with a smile and a *bom dia* as you walk past them, which can be rather disconcerting when you return to the UK and people hurry past you without even making eye contact.

Neighbours will share bags full of fruit and vegetables with you and will be generous and helpful whenever they can be. They will rarely invite you into their home though, and if you are invited in, they usually don't do the British thing of 'let me show you round' or give you a tour of their house. In the UK we have the words house and home which mean different things. I have asked many Portuguese people what the word for home is in Portuguese and they mostly shrug and say *casa* which translates simply as house.

✿ℬ✿ℛ✿

You will always carry a 1-euro coin in your pocket or car ready for the supermarket trolley.

Multibanco cash machines here do much more than just give out cash. You can pay bills online, transfer money to other accounts or even your own PayPal account, buy tickets for concerts, shows, and the cinema, deposit cash and even top up your mobile phone. It's no wonder the person in front of you can be at the machine for ten minutes.

You can withdraw up to 400 euros a day from the Multibanco machine, but you must do it in two instalments of 200 euros, which is the maximum you can withdraw in one transaction. But you can just put your card back in and get another 200 euros. It took us ages to find that out.

Most banks out here open at 8.30 a.m. but close at 3 p.m. Some have an hour for lunch when they are closed too, and unless you are in a big city and are lucky, you will find all the banks are closed at the weekend. It does make taking that soggy cheque in to your branch to be banked or cashed a bit more difficult if you are working.

Many large stores and most shopping centres do not open until 10 a.m. I still get caught out arriving at the door of a store that I need to visit at 9.30 a.m. and must wait until 10 a.m. for the doors to open. Supermarkets usually open at 8 a.m. or 8.30 a.m. Many stores in smaller villages still close on Wednesday afternoons.

If a pharmacy is closed, details of the closest open pharmacy and pharmacies that are open 24 hours a day will be posted on the door. Most pharmacies are run by qualified chemists which means that many medicines can be obtained with the pharmacist's advice and without needing a prescription.

You will not miss Tesco's, the UK weather, grey skies and miserable people … at all!

You will delight in shopping in local markets and picking your own fresh fruit and veg and fish and become accustomed to only being able to buy what is in season.

If you buy a gift in a shop, even a very small village shop, if you tell them it is a present for someone it will usually be gift-wrapped beautifully for you with ribbon and bows free of charge. Most large stores and supermarkets even provide free wrapping paper and ribbon at Christmas beside the tills.

❀৯✿৻❀

Rubbish is often collected daily from large bin areas at the end of most main roads. There are recycling bins in most towns and villages and the Portuguese have bins for many forms of recycling (tins, glass, bottles, plastics, paper and card, batteries, lamps, clothes and even food). You do not have to wheel a large bin out to the front of your house as you do in the UK. We have a bin in the kitchen that only holds food waste, and we recycle everything else into three coloured bins that we have placed out on the balcony outside the kitchen door. We take everything we can down to the recycling bins; and although it is only a small gesture, at least we know we are doing something good for the environment.

The connector on top of a large gas bottle has a green side and a red side. The red side is 'On' and the green side signifies the connection is 'Off'. Yes. I know, I think it should be the other way around too!

Letter boxes are not part of your front door here, they are always a separate box situated on the front wall of your house. Condominiums and apartment blocks usually have one mass of letterboxes at the entrance or central shared area; and if you live in a rural location you may well find that your letterbox is at the beginning of your lane, which might be a mile away from your house.

No-one it would seem has yet invented a design for these letter boxes that does not let in the rain and wind, so if you are like us and often go days before we remember to empty the letter box (the one that is right outside our gate, and which we probably walk past four or five times every day) then if it has been raining all of your post will be soggy and wet. It can take several hours or even a day to dry out, and it always seems to coincide with that all-important letter with a cheque inside it arriving.

Many people in apartment blocks or part-time residents often rent out a postal box in the local post office, ensuring that their mail is neither soggy nor lost.

Old email accounts never actually close … they just keep collecting junk emails … over 8,000 at the last count! (thank you Sky).

✿ઙ✿ର✿

The Portuguese are often late! In the UK you would be invited to a birthday party from 2-5 p.m. so you would arrive at 2 p.m. clutching your present and wishing the host a happy birthday. You would be thinking about leaving again about 4.30 p.m. which would be about the time that your Portuguese friends would be arriving, and expecting you to have the barbecue lit. Their invitation would read 'Come along in the afternoon' and they would stay for the evening. Singing 'Happy Birthday' in Portuguese has the same tune, but obviously has Portuguese words, which can be strange to hear for the first time.

You will probably sleep for England when you first arrive. We've met others who agreed that for the first few months it is quite normal to find yourself sleeping for longer each night or napping during the day ... well that's my excuse anyway!

You will fill up your days so easily that you will begin to wonder how you ever managed to fit a full-time job into your life at all.

You won't feel like you are on holiday, but you will feel different, more relaxed, more easy-going and more likely to 'enjoy the moment' and 'go with the flow'.

You will catch yourself checking the weather forecast for the UK on the news and chortling nearly every day ... and then posting annoying photos of blue skies and sunshine on Facebook ... a lot. You just can't help yourself.

You may start a blog, initially just to keep family and friends informed of what you are doing. I had no idea that our blog would grow into one of the most-read blogs on the Algarve, winning awards and recording almost 100,000 views every year. It has been another wonderful creative outlet for both my writing, Dave's photography, and our love of travel and exploration.

You will find expat forums and related Facebook groups can be a very useful source of information. You will also find that these same forums can be infuriatingly annoying places where people often vent and moan about the very place they have chosen to live.

You will probably live a much simpler, more basic, unhurried, thrifty, generous, expansive, healthy, accepting and forgiving, and grateful life.

And if you are like me ... you will need a good sunscreen!

22

Art and Photography in the Algarve

One of our long-held dreams was about to come true. Both Dave and I have always been creative, me with a paintbrush and easel and Dave with a camera, but this had only ever been a hobby for each of us. We both had a serious interest in our chosen crafts, but with so little time free to be able to put aside, they had remained as just that, simply much-loved hobbies for years.

And now suddenly we were here, full time in the Algarve, and I had a lovely light and bright space for a studio downstairs in our home, and Dave had treated himself to a proper camera when he retired from the Police, along with some professional lenses and lots of other important camera gear.

And we had time, lots of time. Although we did not need to work; we both felt at 54 and 42 years old respectively, that we were both too young to retire, and we both fully intended to see where our talents and creative desires led us. Our hope was that we could work at something we enjoyed, be our own boss, and set up and run a business each as small independent sole traders.

We spent the first winter in our new home honing and testing our skills. Dave had the excellent idea of posting a new photograph every single day on his newly created Facebook business page;

entitled his '365 Project'; and I spent many a happy hour in my studio playing with paint and creating new work. By the time spring came around, Dave had a batch of new photographs, mainly seascapes and landscapes; and I had a total of 24 new paintings all completed and ready for a new home. My Facebook page was also live, and Dave had even had a photograph that had gone viral reaching over 52,000 people in less than 24 hours. We were building a loyal following and people seemed to genuinely like what we were doing.

The plan, therefore, seemed simple, that we should set up and run our own pop-up gallery exhibition. We had never done anything like that before, but we were keen and undeterred by our lack of experience. 'How hard can it be?' we thought to ourselves, although we had no idea where we might host such an event.

Facebook to the rescue. We posted up our ideas and discovered a new friend that turned out to be a real supporter of our work in the years ahead. A local hotel chain contacted us and told us that they loved our work, and could we pop in to meet them and see how we could work together. Vicki Good, Sales and Marketing Manager for the Holiday Inn, was fantastic, we met with her, she showed us an upstairs conference room she said we could use, and we were delighted. The only snag? We couldn't fix anything to the walls!

As optimistic as ever, we excitedly said yes to her offer, and went away scratching our heads and wondering how we would get around that problem. Walls are quite important when you are trying to display art, but undaunted we wandered round a local DIY store for ideas, and Dave, genius that he is, came up with the idea of creating table-top easel boards from the trestle stands used as legs to create folding tables. Add some hardwood fascia and fixings and we were away, and we had 16 tabletop easels ready to showcase 32 individual works. Now all we had to do was set everything up, market and promote it and hope that people showed up.

That was the scariest part of all; we had done all that we could in the weeks leading up to our first Easter exhibition, and everything was set up and ready for the opening night. And then the fears kicked in. Firstly, what if no-one came? Then even worse than that, what if they came and didn't like it, and no-one bought anything?! Creating work in a studio is one thing; but then putting it out there into the public domain and waiting for feedback is a different thing altogether. We held our breath, opened the doors and smiled madly!

Within half an hour, Dave had sold his first framed print, and within the hour I had sold two paintings. We were away, and we fashioned our own little 'happy dance' which we jigged around to after each sale. We usually waited until the happy customer had departed, although I think a few clients might have caught a snatch of our happy little jig!

The end of that first week came quickly and it was time to pack up. We were both amazed with how well we had done, not just in terms of sales, but we had a Visitor's Book full of lovely comments, and we had made many new friends. It was a satisfying feeling, realising that we had created work that other people loved, and that our work would be proudly hung up in lots of new homes, both here in the Algarve, and further afield too. We sold to British, French, Canadian and Dutch people, as well as expats living here. One print even went to Lisbon to be with a Portuguese family. It had been a success. We were delighted - and exhausted.

✿❧✿❧✿

A few months later and we were back setting up again in the same venue, with a whole new batch of work. It really spurred me on to create more new paintings, knowing that we had a genuine outlet for our work, and it was also good to know that we could do this ourselves, without having to rely on a gallery or outside help. We started sending out a monthly newsletter, readership grew to almost 500 subscribers, and I began to be asked to paint commissions for clients. We had launched and we were away.

I started to paint pet portraits thanks to a delightful couple we met during our very first exhibition week, who asked me,

"Can you paint dogs?"

"I don't know," I replied, "I've never tried. But I can try for you and see how it goes."

Winston the Labrador became my first ever pet portrait and the owners were delighted. I have since painted over fifty pet portraits and have come to love trying to capture something of the personality of the animal in my paintings. Dogs, cats, rabbits, chickens, a donkey and even a horse ... I am happy to try to paint any pet!

My love of animals also led to us both supporting the Algarve Dog Show for several years. Dave ran around the ring photographing all the dogs, with the winners and their rosettes and proud owners on the podium, and I offered a pet portrait as a prize for the Best in Show each day. My job during the event was to run our display stand, sell work and paint live. That was a first for me, painting with people watching me. I chose a portrait of a dog that I had started at home in the studio and intended to finish painting over the weekend of the show. My easel was set up, paints laid out, painting propped up and I was happily painting, oblivious to the crowd that formed behind me.

Dave will tell you that I do get quite engrossed when I am painting and have no idea what is happening around me. All was going well until I stepped back, brush in hand, to take a better look at what I had just painted. I had no idea that a man was literally peering over my shoulder to get a closer look at my work. I shot back, bumped into him, and nearly knocked the whole table of paints over. How to make an exhibition at a show! Luckily no harm was done to either the man or my painting ... I obviously checked that the painting was alright first.

Other paintings fared less well, however. After a year or so of working in my studio it was time to have a spring clean of my art space. I am a naturally tidy person, and do not like things lying around, and I had several old canvases and boards stacked in the corner of my studio gathering dust. When I first arrived here and started painting, I had fun experimenting with different surfaces and paints, eventually settling on my now favoured primed art boards. I decided that I did not like the uniformity and pattern that emerges on a traditional canvas, and I had a small pile of old canvases that had various daubs and splashes of colour over them. None of them were important to me, and I put them by the back door of the studio ready to throw away.

"Are you sure you want to get rid of these?" asked Dave as he tripped over them.

"Oh yes," I replied, "they're just old attempts, nothing special, they can all go in the bin."

Off went Dave to the bins with them all tucked under his arm and I thought no more about them.

That is, until the following Sunday at the monthly flea market that comes to town. It is always good to have a walk around and see what is for sale. We nick-named it the 'tat-market' as lots of people place junk on the pavement and hope to sell it, alongside the more traditional market stalls and dubious antiques.

We walked to the end, and at almost the last stall I gasped and laughed, tugging on Dave's arm and pointing to the ground. There, stacked up beside some old records, were my paintings that Dave had thrown in the bin. Well, we had to ask, didn't we?

"How much are the paintings over there?" I asked the stallholder.

"Oh those," he replied airily, "they are fifty euros each. They are by a famous local artist."

Perhaps I shouldn't have thrown them away after all.

✧ၷ✧ၣ✧

Move ahead several years and we are both now firmly established, running our own little businesses legally and profitably. It has been a slow process, as it is hard to make any real money here in the Algarve in our chosen creative professions, but we are both delighted with where we are now and wouldn't change anything. After hosting about ten pop-up exhibitions over a period of six years, we now have regular clients, together with new business and contacts on a regular basis, and lots of creative challenges and events still ahead of us.

I am lucky enough to sell paintings almost before they have dried on the easel, which means that sadly I do not have the inventory or body of new work needed to host and run our own exhibitions any more, and I do miss the excitement of those pop-up events.

I have even had two of my paintings on the front covers of local magazines, which was very exciting. I have been commissioned to paint many different views, and now have my own recognisable style of painting in acrylics, which I self-titled my 'New Wave' style as I could not find anything else similar to my approach to a piece of art. Dave always teases me that I can look at a view or one of his photographs and can instantly 'see' the finished painting in my mind, knowing almost instinctively whether something will work in my style.

It still humbles me to know that people love my work. Dave even photographed a house for rental one day with the rental agent present and spotted one of my paintings on the wall in the lounge, which was a rather surreal moment for him, as the agent commented that she loved the painting, and Dave was able to tell her that his wife had painted it!

I tend not to paint now in the depths of winter, as it does get chilly in my studio; and I gave up trying to paint in the hottest part of the summer, as the paint can actually leave my 'stay-wet' palette on the brush and be dry before I can even reach my easel. So I paint for about eight months of the year, which seems to suit me well.

For fun I also like to design and paint little heart-shaped stones, which are great for decoration, meditation or framing. I was asked by someone at an exhibition once where I sourced my heart stones from; and I made the mistake of telling them that there is a secret beach on the Algarve that has heart-shaped stones (!) ... they believed me and begged me to tell them where it was ... oh dear! Since then the story has become embedded into mythical fantasy and that is what I tell all my customers. As to where they are really from ... now that would be telling!!

⟡∞⟡⟡

There are other challenges associated with painting that we have learnt to tackle over the years. One is the art of packing a painting ready to post. I have often spent several days or even weeks completing a piece for a client and I then have to pack it up and ship it off to them. Dave teases me that each painting is like a baby to me; and I feel responsible for it right until the moment it arrives safely with its new owner. We have perfected the art of bubble wrap and cardboard packing now, and the biggest challenge is often at the post office, where they have a very strict 2kg weight limit for their normal registered parcel post service. I add tracking so that I can watch my babies fly across the world and to reassure clients that their painting is on its way.

Our local post office lady can be rather formidable, and I am always nervous taking a parcel in to her in case I go over the 2kg weight limit. Trying to balance a large wrapped painting on a set of small kitchen scales is rather impossible, so I have mastered the skill of picking up the parcel, holding it in my hands and thinking 'yes that is an OK weight'. It is a very scientific process.

I have never had a problem until one day when I wrapped a slightly larger painting, and Dave said to me,

"Do you think that will be under the 2kg limit? It seems heavier to me."

"Oh yes," I replied confidently, "it will be fine."

I should add at this point that once wrapped, my parcels do look rather formidable, and I have often joked that I am glad that I am not at the receiving end of one of these literal works of art; they must be a nightmare to open, as I do like to use the parcel tape quite liberally! They are not something that I would like to have to unwrap and rewrap.

Off I went to the post office, and stood in the usual long queue, inching forward every ten minutes. Our post lady likes to chat to people, and I am always happy to wait and watch people. Finally at the counter I handed over the parcel; and held my breath as she placed it on the official and rather menacing looking set of scales. '2kg' I thought to myself, 'don't be over 2kg.'

I checked the scales … it was 1.96 kg. I am sure the weight of the stamps she added probably tipped it over the 2kg limit, it was that close! The post lady looked disapprovingly at me as I grinned broadly at her, gathered up my paperwork and skipped out of the post office.

✿౯✿ఴ✿

Dave has firmly established himself as a professional, reliable and talented photographer, with an enviable portfolio of work. He has photographed all over the Algarve, including covering weddings at many fabulous locations, both on the beach and inland. He has been lucky enough to cover several weddings at the incredible Estoi Palace near Faro and has also covered intimate elopement shoots on deserted beaches at sunset. He has been to social events with the rich and famous; photographed fabulous multi-million-pound properties; and had his work grace many of the front covers of local magazines over the past few years.

Not bad for a lad whose first camera was a Kodak Instamatic on his 11th birthday over 50 years ago. He tells the story of how he gleefully scampered around with his new camera proudly taking photographs of anything and everything until his dad finally said to him,

"You do realise that it costs a lot of money to have all these photographs developed, don't you?"

Dave had no idea, he just thought you sent away the film and the pictures were magically posted back to you! Thank goodness for digital cameras now; although I wish that camera equipment was cheaper, or that new gear could be miraculously posted to us free today.

✿౯✿ఴ✿

A conversation with a fellow artist led me onto another new creative path, as she enquired of me,

"How do you always end up with your exhibitions featured in the local paper?"

My reply was simple,

"I send them a press release. Why?"

Her reply was rather illuminating,

"I didn't know you could do that."

So began a new project which grew from my initial idea of helping fellow artists here in the Algarve and ended up with the creation of the Algarve Society of Artists. After only a few months we had a website, over 120 members, and a growing community of artists supporting each other, meeting and exhibiting together, and attempting to raise the profile of creativity here in the Algarve.

I also began my first foray into self-publishing, creating a total of six quarterly online art magazines. The first edition had 118 pages, which challenged me into learning how to use InDesign and online publishing sites. They were all well received and enjoyable to create.

My efforts were even rewarded with a rather prestigious award from the local Rotary Club here in the Algarve, who surprised me with their 'Entrepreneur of the Year' award in 2018. It was a real shock and a lovely honour.

I handed over the Society to fellow journalist friends last year, and it is still going strong. It felt good to be able to create something that could help and support other artists out here.

We have also made so many friends through our own creative journey, and have met people from all over the world, and from so many different walks of life, both residents and visitors here in the Algarve. We also know that our work is displayed in private homes and businesses in so many different countries, which is a real thrill and honour. It is hard to believe looking back on that first exhibition all those years ago in the Holiday Inn hotel, that we would be where we are today, and we will always be grateful to them for believing in us and giving us our first big break.

23

Kat the Dog

I t would be fair to say that I have wanted a dog for a long while; I grew up with always having a dog as part of the family and adore the love and companionship they give you. There are so many rescue dogs out here that need a home that it was always going to be a dog in need that would win us both over, but the question was … which one?

Having talked to our friend Ginie from the SOS Algarve Animals (SOSAA) charity about this, we initially toyed with the idea of adopting a young puppy, but it was good to talk things through first and we agreed that a puppy would be a large commitment when we are both working and would be harder to fit into our lives than we first thought. We happily left it to Ginie, and she promised that she would find us the right dog.

Almost a year passed by and it is funny how things turn out to have their own sense of timing. Ginie managed to get herself a much-needed holiday to see friends in Spain, her dedication to the charity and the rescue dogs is immense, and all consuming, so this was a rare chance to leave the kennels behind and travel. She tells the story of how she was driving down a main road in a remote village near Seville when this poor scrap of a dog came into view running down the road. Ginie stopped her car, whistled and the dog promptly jumped into the back of her car and curled up on the seat. More amused than anything that on her weekend away she had managed to rescue another dog, she continued to her friends' house and fed the dog, who was in a pretty poor state.

The next morning, probably as a result of being fed, the dog started to produce milk from her teats, which is when they realised that she had recently had pups. A trip back to the exact place that she had been found did not produce any reaction at all from her; and a visit to the local vet confirmed that she was in such a poor state of health that she would have given birth to still-born pups at best.

The first photos taken of her, who was now called Olalya after the place she was found, are quite sad to see, although the sweet nature of this little dog was already evident. It was obvious that Ginie had quite fallen for her and her gentle ways, as she curled up on the back seat of the car alongside Ginie's own personal pet dog Cheeky, and happily began her new adventure into a foreign country and new life.

The charity does a marvellous job when they find a rescue dog, as every dog is taken to the vets, checked and chipped, vaccinated and nursed back to health if necessary, and critically, sterilised. You can be sure that when you have a dog through SOSAA that you know what you are getting. They are checked to see how they are with other dogs and cats, and children, and they work in close collaboration with local vets at every stage of the process.

Olalya's coat was in such a bad state that she had to have all her fur shaved down, which made her look even more forlorn, but still lovely, with chocolate-coloured eyes that said so much about her life. We saw the photos of her on Facebook and I was immediately drawn to her and kept going back to her page and story. It was no surprise then when Ginie called me up and said,

"I have just the dog for you."

I immediately replied,

"I know, I have seen her already."

We both knew we were talking about the same dog.

Dave and I arranged to go over and meet Olalya, and she was the dearest little thing, skinny but happy, quiet but interested in us; and she settled down beside us whilst we talked things through with Ginie. We had agreed before we went to see her that we would go away and talk about it afterwards and take our time deciding, but I fell for her instantly and Dave later admitted the same thing. It was quite emotional driving away as she trotted up quietly to the gates as we drove out and stood looking up after us as we left.

We rang up the next morning of course and agreed that initially we would foster her with a view to adoption. It is great that the charity offers this option as it meant we could have a few weeks with her with no pressure or permanent commitment; giving time for her … and us … to settle and see how things went. It had been a long while since I had had a dog and we knew that it would be a big commitment and lifestyle change for us, and one that we felt ready for.

Two days later we were back to collect her, and she recognised us straight away and it was exciting to be able to fill in the papers and pick up her lead and take her home in our car. We were like proud new parents driving her home, she was still quite underweight and a little nervous, but had sweet trusting eyes that took everything in.

Taking her home and introducing her to everything was quite something as she was initially wary and shy of so many things; her reflection in the shiny oven door made her run; she wouldn't go down stairs or anywhere near our basement stairs as they were going down into the unknown; she walked round drain covers (still does!) and seagulls overhead made her scarper! But slowly and patiently I worked quietly with her over several days and the transformation was almost instant. If something spooked her, I spent time with her reassuring her and settling her. Now she stops and looks at herself in a mirror (!) she sits and watches birds and even planes fly overhead, and she made herself at home in her new bed in the kitchen straight away and created her own little routine of 'perimeter checks' of the garden each morning, scampering up and down the steps without a second thought.

Her given name by the charity, Olalya, which was taken from the nearby name of the village she was found, was not an easy name to pronounce; and we thought long and hard about what to name her, toying with several ideas. Dave has a great Monty Python sense of humour though and has always wanted to have 'a dog called cat', so that's what we ended up calling her … Kat. Initially it seemed a bit daft, but now it seems to suit her, she's a quirky little girl, and it fits her well. So Kat the dog she is!

The first time we took her to a beach was amusing, we doubt that she had ever seen the sea or sand before, and she was a little unsure; however now she adores the beach, romping around, digging holes in the sand, and playing with us and other dogs if she meets them. She is mostly a Spanish water dog, with some poodle thrown in there for good measure apparently, but she doesn't seem to like water very much! If there is a puddle on the ground she will walk around it, and although sometimes she does decide to go for a little paddle in the sea, she is not a great fan of swimming unless there is a nice calm river of water with a gentle slope in and out, and it is a hot day and she wants to cool off.

The day she went head-first into our friend's fishpond was hilarious as she just didn't even recognise that the green stretch of something ahead of her was a pond of water. In she plopped, and came out slightly bemused, dripping wet but none the worse for her experience.

We did take her to the village of Alte one afternoon which has a lovely river beach with a gentle slope down to the water. And ducks. Did I mention that Kat adores birds of all kinds, including ducks? Off she scampered into the water, had a lovely paddle around, said hello to the ducks (she is very gentle, there is no hint of aggression in her, she just wanted to say hello) and then out she climbed, soaking wet and happy. Sadly for the contingent from a local coach tour that had just turned up, who had filed out of their coach and were all stood at the side of the river holding their cameras aloft, she made a beeline for them.

Initially there was lots of 'ooh-ing' and 'aah-ing' and someone saying,

"Isn't that a pretty dog?"

And then Kat decided that in front of the whole group was the perfect location to have a shake. She has a nice big fluffy coat in the winter, and it holds a lot of water. And I mean a lot of water. Which landed in giant droplets all over the whole group. They all disappeared rather quickly back into their coach. I have no idea why!

✿ʂᎾ✿Ꮭ✿

It was a very easy decision to turn fostering into full adoption and she is now registered, chipped and has all the necessary paperwork and passport and is officially ours. SOSAA were great all the way through this, giving us advice and help, meeting us at the vets, and guiding us through the process. It's Portugal, of course it's a paper trail of every imaginable required piece of paper and forms in triplicate, but it was not too complicated, and the charity were there at every step to help us. They also gave us sensible advice about diet and the required jabs and precautions on how to make sure she is protected against all sorts of diseases and illnesses. She now has a Scalibor collar and monthly Activyl and Milbemax treatments and annual jabs. In Portugal you must also protect against rabies, and it's all recorded in the pet passport which seems to be a sensible system.

We have her registered both at the vets and at the local Junta de Freguesia ... of course there was more than one system to register a dog, what did you expect?! The vets register the microchip in the SIRA database, and the Junta register it on a separate SICAFE database. They have recently started to merge the two databases, but our local vet has also kept the details on the old system too, just in case.

The Junta also issues an annual certificate which is a stamped and certified piece of A4 paper, which we must always carry along with her passport. The irony is that she has almost as many papers to carry as we do, and I have joked that my handbag is now the size of a weekend-away rucksack living out here!

What the SOSAA Charity failed to warn us about was just how much we would fall in love with this little scruffy scrap of a dog. She really is the sweetest, gentlest, most content and well behaved little girl; happy to be around us, curled up on the old sofa in my studio while I paint, or out walking on a beach or local village, field or cliff-top with us; or even sat patiently beside Dave while he is out photographing on a beach somewhere. She now sleeps on my bed and I love seeing her little contented face snuggled up on a pillow at night, snuffling gently away to herself in her sleep. Her life now must seem a world away from the street-sleeping scavenging existence she knew before in Spain.

She has gained all the weight she needs to and has transformed from the little scrap we met into a healthy and happy dog. Crucially she has also gained strength and power in her legs and body too, she can now easily manage a long beach walk in the morning and another one in the afternoon, which is great as we are always out and about somewhere and it is lovely to have some company of the four-legged variety. She also charms everyone she meets as she is so gentle and placid; if we meet friends for lunch at a restaurant, she will sit by my feet under the table outside for over two hours with not a murmur or any fuss at all.

She is known and loved by all in the village, they call her *Ovelha* (little sheep), and she has several local people who all manage to sneak her a biscuit when I am not looking! She has an instinct for knowing exactly where Sandra the street cleaner is in the village and will go scampering up to her for a dog chew. She has her own Facebook Page and regularly gets her own invitations out to dinner at our friends' house, the invite usually mentions that we can come too as an afterthought somewhere near the end of the message.

It's been lovely watching her personality blossom, she's a very contained and content little thing, and doesn't jump up or lick madly or go wild, (thank goodness) but her little stump of a tail and her whole bum wags when she is happy, she now puts a paw on your shoulder to give you a hug if you fuss her, and if you pull out a burr from her fur (which is a daily task as she seems to collect the things for a pastime) then she gently licks your hand as if to say 'thank you'. She is also bright as a button, doesn't miss a thing, loves routine and instinctively seems to know so much, and she adores mashed up sardines on her dinner and sleeping upside down!

We cannot thank SOSAA enough, not only for finding Kat, but also for the amazing work they do, both in rescuing and re-homing dogs and cats, but also for their ongoing and pro-active sterilisation campaigns. The problem of strays and litters of unwanted kittens and puppies continues on a daily basis out here; in one weekend during a February Sterilisation Campaign the charity sterilised 46 cats and dogs, with 90% of the animals being female from all areas of the Algarve and at a cost of 1,500 euros. All of this of course requires funding and donations for a charity who work tirelessly and patiently to make a difference.

For several years I gave a percentage of my profits from all of my Pet Portrait paintings to the charity; and even a small donation can be used by them, and any promotion and support we can give them can only help them to continue the valuable work that they do.

And every time I look at Kat's beautiful face, I am grateful for the day that Ginie stopped and whistled a little scruffy scrap of fur into the back seat of her car.

24

Abandoned Animals

S adly not all dogs and cats on the Algarve are as lucky as Kat the dog. Not a week goes by that I do not see another new abandoned dog around the village, most are hungry, neglected and often ill. Many are just dumped by owners who no longer want the responsibility, cost or time involved in looking after a pet.

We had a beautiful yet sad young male dog hiding around the local beach of Pintadinho for months. The story goes that he was with a German couple in a motorhome parked around the local area for the winter. March came and off they went, literally abandoning the poor dog, leaving him behind as they drove away. The dog was so distraught he had not left the beach and surrounding village area since that day, and he was often to be found sat on the beach in the early morning light howling and crying. He skirted around the edge of the beach shying away from all human contact. A generous local lady fed him every day and it took her weeks and weeks of gentle patience on her part for him to even begin to trust her. Finally he trusted her enough to let her approach him, and so began the long process of reintegrating him.

Other dogs appear to be better treated, as many local people have at least one dog, kept solely as protection for their home and garden. However closer inspection will show that some are tethered to a desperately short rope or chain, and others have the freedom of the garden but are never walked or fussed. We have a neighbour nearby who has recently acquired a rather sweet yet timid male dog, a sort of basset hound crossed with a beagle. Every day they leave for work and leave the gates to their property wide open, and Henry as we have affectionately named him, is free to roam as he pleases all day and night. He is sadly completely uneducated when it comes to having any basic road sense at all; we live on a reasonably busy main road; and he is often to be found sat in the middle of the road, staring into space oblivious to the traffic swerving round him.

Other neighbours are more exasperating. One family have had a young male dog for about three years now who can jump their front wall and scamper off down the road barking at the sky. He is another hopeless case when it comes to road sense, however this fella is somewhat faster on his feet and skips merrily down the road avoiding all vehicular obstacles as he goes. As is not unusual out here, he has not been sterilised. This seems to be a particularly moot point out here between local animal rescue charities who vehemently advocate sterilisation as soon as possible, and you cannot blame them, with the large numbers of unwanted puppies and kittens that appear with alarming regularity across the area; and the owners who state that they cannot 'take his balls away, he won't be a "man" anymore'. Or they confidently claim that their female dog cannot be done yet as 'she wants to have puppies'.

Our neighbours decided that our little well-endowed and firmly intact hero needed some company and brought home a young female puppy. Surprise surprise, after less than a year, she came into season. Picture the scene outside their house if you will, it was like something out of Lady and the Tramp, with an ever-growing line of young eager male dogs all lined up outside their gate, all clutching bouquets of flowers, boxes of chocolates, and theatre tickets for two, to woo our fair maiden. Well it was a little rowdier and noisier than that, and the hopeful suitors were not exactly standing in an orderly queue ... although they were all serenading our young heroine.

Our neighbour's response to all this unwanted male attention?

She placed a pair of young girl's pants over our modest maiden's virtuosity. A pair of pants ... I kid you not. And they were bright red too. Well, they might as well have had 'come and get it here boys' written all over them too in sparkling glitter. But our dear neighbour genuinely believed that this measure would be enough to stop anything untoward happening to her young fair four-legged and petrified pup. It hardly needs the punchline adding does it? The requisite number of weeks later, and there were nine more puppies in the world to find homes for. Amusingly some of them looked exactly like ... yes, you've guessed it ... their other dog. He was having none of the competition and got on with the job in hand himself as soon as he got wind of her condition. The only amazing thing in all of this is their genuine surprise that he would do such a thing.

Other abandoned dogs do better and find a new loving home to enjoy. We have a scruffy yet endearing little chap that lives happily in someone's front garden since being abandoned by another family. The new owners are happy to feed him and keep him healthy and up to date at the vets, however they too work all day and he is left to roam the streets. He has perfected the art of running alongside moving cars barking crazily at them as they drive by. Locals are used to him by now and don't bat an eyelid at him, however unsuspecting motorists are less fortunate and tend to try to break or swerve to miss the small 'Usain Bolt' four legs hurtling along beside them.

I have named him Charlie, and he is quite a sweetie, always affectionate and pleased to see me. Chatting to another local person on the estate where he lives one day, I discovered that they call him Chewbacca and he has friends all over the place that keep him entertained and well fed. I met the actual family that own him one day and they called him by a completely different name, and I was quite shocked.

"Oh no, he's called Charlie ... Or Chewbacca!" I said.

Evidently, he has several useful aliases, which no doubt will come in handy when the police try to issue him with a speeding ticket.

✿ℬ✿ℛ✿

There are several shelters and many rescue charities across the Algarve, most of whom seem to be full to bursting point with rescued and abandoned animals. The charities rely solely on donations, support and volunteers, and many take on the cases no-one else wants.

Behind each charity you have an enormous amount of work done by people who are mostly all volunteers (both expats and Portuguese) who take care of the animals in the shelter, take them to the vet so that they can be sterilised and checked over, walk them, organise adoptions fairs and other adoption events, visit houses before re-homing, follow up on adoptions and crucially fund-raise so that all of this work can happen. Education is also critical alongside the sterilisation programmes, which are often targeted at street cats and dogs, and low-paid families who want to ensure their pets cannot produce litters or puppies, and who don't want to resort to a small red pair of pants as protection.

In October 2014 the Portuguese Government introduced laws that made the mistreatment or abandonment of pets a crime, punishable with hefty fines or prison sentences. The GNR Police has a special unit SEPNA unit dedicated to the protection of the environment and the enforcement of environmental laws, including cruelty to animals. However so much more needs to be done than simply passing laws.

The most bizarre law of all that came into force at the end of October 2019 has to be the law that stated that all pet owners will have to register their dogs, cats and ferrets in a new computerised pet information system that was launched nationwide. Dogs have always had to be registered but adding cats, and hilariously, ferrets to the list just made me smile.

Many Portuguese people do not have a name for their animals, even their dogs, but I doubt any of them have a name for their ferret. I can just see them arriving at their local Junta building to register their pet and being asked,

"Name of ferret?"

The system is designed apparently to assist with the

'identification and registration of pets', so presumably the next question would be,

"Does your ferret have any distinguishing marks or scars or tattoos?"

Thank goodness they didn't decide to create a national pet passport with this initiative, complete with photograph. I can just picture a grinning ferret sat in a photo booth wondering which is his or her best side for a photograph. And no, before you ask, Dave does not specialise in ferret photography ...

25

The Village That Came Back to Life

This story of a little village on the Algarve that has been brought back to life is a remarkable one. A high-flying executive from Lisbon who fell in love with a run-down and dilapidated village and promptly sold up everything he owned, took early retirement, bought virtually the entire village and moved to live there with his family. That was in 2006, and the transformation that has been made to the little village of Pedralva is nothing short of incredible.

The before and after pictures in the reception area of this resort tell the story of its renovation so well, and there are still some ruined properties in the village waiting to be developed, which gives you a sense of the scale of the project António Ferreira undertook when he decided to bring this beautiful little village back to life.

Pedralva was once a thriving little traditional Portuguese village, but by 2006 there were only 9 inhabitants left in the village, and now there are 31 fully restored houses which you can stay in for a short break or longer holiday. The houses nestle alongside a handful of privately owned houses and sit comfortably beside the locals who still live there and the local farms that surround the village.

Most of the long-forgotten and dilapidated properties had been left abandoned for so long that tracing the owners and purchasing the properties was no easy task. One sale involved gathering the signatures of no less than 28 owners. António Ferreira initially bought two small houses, then 12 more, and he now owns over 30.

Aside from his own 4million euros budget, plus an investment of 1 million euros by Vila do Bispo local Council; it took several years, a great deal of labour and a lot of love to restore the village. António was careful to retain as many of the original designs and layouts of the properties as possible; and to use authentic and traditional materials and techniques, so that the traditional rustic style was maintained.

All the houses have been decorated and furnished in a traditional Portuguese style, but also with comfort in mind. Each property has 1, 2 or 3 bedrooms, a living room, kitchenette and bathroom. Each house is a separate unit, and some also have a small garden area with barbecue, ensuring privacy.

All the houses have white walls with different colourful doors and windows, which adds to the sense of being part of a greater whole and ties the whole village together.

Pedralva is now listed as a Touristic Village. It has a gourmet grocery in the same location as the former village store; the reception area also runs a snack-bar, they have a summer store called 'Pedralva Outlet' and they have two restaurants which are already famous on the Costa Vicentina coast: 'Pizza Pazza Pizzeria' and 'Sitio da Pedralva'.

The old primary school building has also been converted into a communal space, perfect for meetings, courses and classes. This is a wonderful base from which to enjoy the local landscape, villages and beaches that are nearby.

The village has also promoted various sporting events including the WQS - World Surf Algarve competition and the MTB National mountain bike Marathon Cup. They also host regular craft fairs in the streets of the village in the summer.

You will find Pedralva nestled in the Algarvian countryside, near the stunning array of west coast beaches that we love so much. Find Vila do Bispo on the map and then follow the signs through some beautiful open landscape, with pine trees, farms and green fields.

Look out for the brown tourist sign for the village as it is easy to miss! Somehow the air seems to feel fresher, the sky just a little brighter and the view just a little more beautiful as you approach the narrow lanes that lead down to the village, which nestles into the surrounding fields so perfectly.

✿ຖ✿ଯ✿

We were invited to spend a weekend at the village, staying in one of the renovated houses, and experiencing the real Pedralva. It was a most generous offer by the owner, and we were delighted to accept.

We arrived and found the car parking which is at the edge of the village. We parked up next to an old bright red VW camper van and instantly realised that this would be a different holiday with a slower, gentler pace in a relaxed venue, and then a smile spread easily across our faces as we looked round.

We were warmly greeted at reception and given the keys to our little house for the weekend, which was named 'Barranco' and off we went to excitedly explore this quaint little place.

The houses have all been beautifully restored in a traditional and sympathetic way, with carefully chosen mis-matched furniture which just seems right in such a property.

The bathroom was fabulous, with a big walk-in cave for a shower, and the first surprise was the modern steaming hot water that came out from the taps and the big fluffy towels. It was luxury hidden within a simple interior.

Our bedroom was tucked up in the eaves and was enormous. Lovely crisp bedding and more quaint furniture and furnishings, including a proper old Singer sewing machine sat on a table.

The kitchen area was very well equipped with a little oven, electric hob, microwave and plenty of utensils, cutlery and crockery. We even had an espresso machine; the simple exterior of our little house really did belie its interior comforts.

The one big difference here is that there is no television. And no internet! And very little mobile phone reception. They have free wi-fi in the reception area if you are desperate. After about five minutes we relaxed on the comfy sofa, and just sat and talked.

We then went off to explore the little village which is charming. Little cobbled paths lead to each of the houses and wind their way around the village and add to the overall charm of the location.

We wandered around corners, enchanted by the little hidden houses and views, and then arrived at a BBQ area and pizza/bread oven with shared seating, and the most stunning views of the local countryside. We could see the local farm nearby, they had sheep grazing in the field, with views of neatly arranged vegetable plots, and flowers in abundance. The overall sense was one of solitude and a tranquillity rarely found even on the Algarve.

The aim of the resort is a simple one – to give guests an authentic experience of 'living in the past', of living in a real village, with space, peace and quiet. It is the perfect location for families and children to take time away together, and for people tired from the frantic pace of modern life. It is a space to step aside, refresh and revive yourself, and recharge your batteries.

Or perhaps not! If it all seems too quiet for you then talk to reception and book a trek or hire a bike or go for a nature walk. You can go horse-riding or book a surfing lesson on a nearby beach. Pedralva prides itself on being a Tourism Village and it has excellent links with many local companies and activities.

There is a shared community pool, a games room with a pool table, bicycle rentals, and equipment for mountain biking and hiking, snorkelling and other activities related to sports, nature, and the coast, all for hire.

Or you could just grab a coffee from the restaurant as we did and sit outside in the sunshine or the reception area and relax. If you are lucky, the owner's Newfoundland dog will amble over for some fuss. 'Urso' (the Bear) is aptly named!

Breakfast the next morning was a lovely spread of continental breakfast with bread rolls, croissants, ham, cheese, jams and spreads. We were also asked if we wanted scrambled egg which was then freshly cooked, but the best part was the freshly squeezed orange juice which tasted amazing and the big jugs of coffee. A yoghurt to finish and we were set for the day of exploring the nearby beaches.

There are two eateries on site at Pedralva and the main restaurant is called 'Sítio da Pedralva'. It is a small, friendly place with mis-matched glasses and a simple decor with white painted school furniture but do not let that fool you. We had an amazing meal at a very reasonable price. There is also an outside eating area too, the menu choices were very good, and the staff were attentive and entertaining.

❀ ⅋ ❀ Ϟ ❀

Bringing this village back to life has also regenerated the local area and local businesses. The local 'Pizza Pazza' restaurant was already on site and now it is thriving. We had to try it out of course and we were reliably advised to book a table in advance, which seemed rather strange to us as the resort was very quiet when we stayed there early in the season, but at about 6.30 p.m. the cars started appearing and by 8.30 p.m. the place was full!

There is a cosy inside seating area, where you can end up sat next to local people, surfers, business people from Lisbon on holiday, or if you are very lucky … Prince William, who has previously enjoyed a meal here whilst surfing nearby. They also have an upstairs outside terrace with more seating for you to enjoy the setting sun and magnificent views from.

The pizza place is very informal, the menu was simple and the wine choice even simpler, as you could only choose between red or white wine in a jug. Our waiter smilingly described the red wine as,

"smooth, fruity and guaranteed not to give you a hangover."

There was a wide choice of pizza toppings and the menu has some fantastically named pizzas including the 'Cannibal' and the 'Jungle'. They even had a matching 'Tarzan and Jane' combo; and an amusing translation of house salad as 'salad in the way of the house.'

We ordered a herb and garlic bread starter, which was great, it was very well-seasoned and flavoured and it disappeared rather quickly! We also had olives and *tremoços* (lupini) beans too.

I had ordered a Tropical pizza complete with pineapple and banana, and Dave had a seafood pizza covered in anchovies, and both came out piping hot and full of topping. Dave's pizza was so big it overlapped his dinner plate!

The staff were great, very friendly and amusing and obviously proud of their little gem to which people travel far and wide to visit.

Pudding was an easy choice for me as the magic word tiramisu was on the menu. It didn't disappoint either, it was light and moist and wonderful.

The Pizza Pazza is open from Tuesday to Saturday at 6 p.m. and on Sundays they open at 1 p.m. They didn't seem to have a published closing time and knowing the laid-back style of the venue it would probably be open until the last person gave up eating!

Overall, we had a great evening, surrounded by friendly people, eating good simple food which was well-cooked and well presented. We left full and happy and determined to return soon.

On our last morning we were lucky enough to be able to meet António Ferreira and spend time talking to him about the remarkable transformation that he has made to this special village, and the concept that is Pedralva. He is a warm, engaging, gentle and articulate man, who is passionate about this project and he has big plans for the future too.

His vision was simple – to combine the past and the future by weaving together the culture, community and history of this beautiful village and to provide a genuine and authentic holiday experience of village life.

We found all the staff at the resort to have mastered the art of being present and helpful without being conspicuous. If you need anything, someone is there to help you and give you advice. It is indeed a gentle place to stay, and we thoroughly enjoyed our time at Pedralva.

We left feeling relaxed, de-stressed and content. The sky was blue, the flowers were in full bloom, the sun was shining and Pedralva left us feeling that all was indeed well with the world.

26

How Much Does it Cost to Live Here?

I thought it might be useful to try to address a question we are often asked and which we found very difficult to find information on before we bought our house - 'how much does it actually cost to live here in Portugal?'

Although it is difficult to generalise and the costs will be different in each case, depending on a number of factors, all we wanted to try to find out in advance were some ballpark figures to give us an idea how much things cost, and especially how expensive it would be to have a house over here. In other words would the budget we had available be enough for us to live on.

I sighed to myself the other day reading a Facebook forum post where the writer asked on behalf of some friends if 3,000 US Dollars a month would be enough money to live on in the Algarve, as their friends had 'fallen on hard times' and were concerned this would not be sufficient to live on. At the current exchange rate that equates to about 2,750 euros a month, whereas the average Portuguese person survives on a salary of around 800 euros a month, and the minimum wage salary is currently only 630 euros a month.

Perspective is everything and of course it depends on the type of lifestyle you are looking for. The writer's friends might not be able to afford to rent a villa with a pool in what is known as the 'Golden Triangle' area or live a luxurious lifestyle on that budget; but they sure can lead a good life out here on that amount of money.

If you are looking for a simple life, eating local produce, going out to eat locally, driving a 'normal' car and either renting or purchasing an average sized house or apartment, then the Algarve is certainly affordable. Rent here is higher than in other areas of Portugal (excluding Lisbon and Porto); and it can be hard to find a long-term rental property in the main tourist areas as many owners like to rent their property out on a weekly basis through the summer months. But if you are happy to move slightly further out away from the main beach resorts; then you can find something to rent for around 600 - 700 euros a month.

Bills are difficult to compare as it depends on the size of the property and number of occupants. Many houses do not have mains gas, so you must buy gas bottles. Large bottles can last anything from only five weeks in the depths of winter to twelve weeks in the summer and cost around 80 - 100 euros a bottle.

Electricity costs are comparable with the UK, as is petrol, which is much more expensive here than Spain. Many people that live in the far eastern stretch of the Algarve drive over to Spain to fill up their cars and buy their gas bottles.

As mentioned previously, cars are very expensive to purchase out here, and many Portuguese people lease their vehicles. An annual road tax for vehicles varies depending on the vehicle type. A small five door low emissions vehicle will cost about 35 euros a year to tax. Car insurance varies depending on whether you want the minimum third-party insurance that most local people have, or fully comprehensive insurance if you can get it, which can cost anything from 200 - 400 euros a year.

Public transport is cheap, with one-way tickets on buses and metros starting from around 1.50 euros and booking a train fare in advance can reap huge savings.

Many people like to have air-conditioning for the summer months in their property, and this can easily double or even triple the electricity bill. An average electric bill of around 80 - 100 euros a month can suddenly easily reach over 200 euros a month in the summer. If you have a swimming pool, unless you can run it completely on solar power (which is possible) then expect your pool to cost you at least another 100 euros a month in electricity.

I am always astounded that more properties out here do not harness the potential of solar energy, although we do know of a few friends that manage to live almost solely 'off-grid'. It is unusual though.

There is no equivalent of council tax to pay on rental properties, although if you buy a house, you will need to pay a property owner tax, or IMI each year. The rate is calculated on the value of the property, but some properties are valued at a rate going back to around 1955 (or so it seems). We have friends that have an old property and they only pay about 80 euros a year property tax (!), however the average for a three-bedroom house in an urban area would be about 600 euros a year.

Private Medical Insurance can range from around 600 to well over 2,000 euros per person per year, and some prescription items which would be free in the UK (e.g. statins, hydrocortisone, thyroxine, etc) are expensive to buy over here. Many expats seem to mix and match private medical insurance with public services. If you have access to the general healthcare system, then your prescriptions are subsidised.

If you are working, especially self-employed you will also have to pay social security in Portugal, in order for you to access healthcare, education and other state services. This is priced according to income earned, and now starts at a flat rate of 20 euros a month, even if you do not declare any earnings at all that month. Add to that higher tax rates on earnings and the advice and guidance of a good accountant cannot be over-emphasised here. There are Non-Habitual Residency schemes and Golden Visas, and specialist advisers are required in order to access things correctly.

It is also sensible to factor in household costs like maintenance and re-painting of your property too. The average cost for a medium size house to be re-painted outside is about 4,500 euros and will last

5-7 years if you are lucky, depending on the condition and location of the property.

When it comes to food and entertainment, this is of course determined by your lifestyle. If you are happy to 'live like the Portuguese', buying your food from the market and local stores, eating fresh healthy food and drinking local wine: 1.50 euros will get you a nice bottle of wine; and if you eat out where the locals eat, then you can live a relatively cheap and comfortable life.

If you buy everything at large foreign supermarkets, shop online back to the UK and have items shipped out here, and eat out in tourist area restaurants and bars, play a lot of golf, or have a boat moored in the marina, then Portugal can soon become an expensive place to live.

The difference between the two lifestyles can be simply summed up as follows:

Our local Portuguese café has a constant special offer on the board, you can buy an espresso and a *pastel de nata* cake for 1.20 euros. It's a difficult offer to refuse! Dave went off to do a photo shoot at a posh resort complex in the 'Golden Triangle' area and he arrived early, so he went into a local café at the resort and ordered an espresso and *pastel de nata*. The bill came, and Dave gasped when he read 7.50 euros.

"Are you sure this is right?" he asked the waitress.

"Oh yes," she replied, smiling broadly. "It's our special offer at the moment, only 7.50 euros."

Dave wasn't brave enough to ask how much it usually costs, but he made sure he swept up every crumb on his plate before he left.

It really is about perceptions and lifestyle choices out here. You can live simply and gently and survive on a reasonable amount of money. Or you can live the high life if you can afford to.

Overall I think things are not much different here than a few years ago, although we used to enjoy an amazingly good exchange rate for the British pound against the euro and now prices seem to have risen alongside other UK prices, however the overall comments I have received from friends are similar to the following:

"We don't live an extravagant life, but we do very much enjoy life."

"Luxury lifestyle? No, but we enjoy ourselves and don't really stint on what we buy."

We will continue to lead a simple life and order our coffee and cake in the local café.

27

The Risk of Fire

The headline read 'Fires Rage Across the Algarve' and even reached the national news in the UK. Publicity drives, reminders not to throw cigarette stubs, and a ban on private garden or commercial fires is sadly not enough to stop fires from starting here. Other causes are more difficult to predict, including overhead electricity cables catching fire. Sadly it would also appear that the fires are sometimes started deliberately, which is a terrible thing. The penalty for such a crime never seems to fit, not when you consider that this dangerous act can put lives, homes and businesses at serious risk.

We have witnessed the devastation that a forest fire can cause here in the Algarve several times from a distance. The beautiful regions of Fóia, Monchique, Alferce and Caldas de Monchique that we can see from our house have all suffered from raging fires causing devastation and destruction in their wake. However it was all a bit too close for comfort one summer, as the fires at Fóia and Monchique raced uncontrollably close to our friends' house.

The top of Fóia is such a majestic and peaceful place, it is hard to imagine such a spectacular place ravaged by flames; but we could see the fire spreading throughout the evening and night from our balcony. Such was the force of the blaze you could see the eucalyptus trees exploding, sending sparks of flame shooting out into the landscape and setting off more fires. The speed in which it moves was also frightening, and almost impossible to control when trees explode so suddenly like this. There has been much debate raging about the eucalyptus planting across Portugal, and politics and profit do not sit comfortably together in this context.

What never fails to amaze us with such incidents is the sheer bravery of the Bombeiros (Fire Brigade), and the kindness and generosity of both local and expat people who come together to support the firefighting. The Bombeiros are an amazing bunch of people, although we were quite horrified to realise that only approximately 10% of the staff are actually paid staff; and that the remaining 90% are all local volunteers. When a major series of fires like this break out, there is often insufficient protective gear to go around, and many Bombeiros end up fighting in their normal clothes. Crews are on standby and travel from all over Portugal to assist in an incident of this scale, and the crews work tirelessly and through the night often for several days to try to control the flames.

The local support for the Bombeiros is rightly justified, and we have been heartened to see how many local people rally round to collect vital items for them. They always need small bottles of water, energy bars, energy drinks, snacks and fruit, socks and towels during an emergency.

You can drop them off at any fire station; however we have discovered an excellent Facebook group and charity that report on the current fires and co-ordinate the collection and distribution of the resources called the Associação Alerta de Incêndio Florestal / Forest Fire Alert. Our hats go off to all the volunteers that give up their time and travel around collecting and delivering, and to Debby Burton, the President of the charity group, for organising it all. Other members are also willing to store items for the Bombeiros as they often sadly do not have the storage facilities available to stockpile the necessary items - hence the rapid response required by local people when an incident occurs.

We were delighted to read that Debby Burton was recently

awarded the British Empire Medal for 'services to the community in the Algarve, Portugal' which is indeed a well-deserved award. Her work and fund-raising through the Facebook group is tireless, allowing many stations to receive proper kit for the firefighters to wear, as well as providing the supplies and information support required for each incident in the region.

Other charities like Operation Florian, which is a UK charity set up by British fire-fighters to save lives overseas by donating reconditioned fire engines and emergency equipment to the world's poorest regions, have even donated equipment and clothing to our firefighters here. Recently South Yorkshire Fire and Rescue donated a huge batch of equipment to the Albufeira Bombeiros worth 150,000 euros following their devastating floods in Albufeira. The local chief of fire staff described it as the 'biggest donation the fire station has seen in 30 years'.

The Portuguese National Authority for Civil Protection also have a website that lists all current fire incidents and gives useful advice to residents and visitors alike. The Safe Communities Portugal project and the Secretary of State for Civil Protection created a leaflet 'Safe Village – Safe People'[1] that covers a number of important topics including the action to take if a fire approaches your home; what to do if you get surrounded by a fire; if you are near a fire; if you are confined inside a building, and the action required in case of evacuation. For those living in high risk areas the recommendation is to have an evacuation kit ready and available. It was a sobering read when we were handed a copy at a local community event, although it is always better to be informed and prepared.

Although this may sound dramatic and alarmist, it is a fact that fires have been gradually encroaching into rural and populated areas over the last few years, and the authorities have changed their terminology from describing them as 'forest fires' to 'rural fires'.

In some high-risk villages, mainly north of the A22 motorway which runs along the Algarve, awareness sessions have also been conducted by the municipal civil protection and GNR (local police), showing escape routes and assembly points should a fire break out.

At its height that summer, the fires at Fóia alone had over 350 firefighters, 100 fire engines and 9 air support tackling the blaze, and sadly that was only one of several fires blazing at the same time. In total over 1,000 firefighters were reported as battling the flames in the region, which consumed more than 1,000 hectares of land.

Householders in the area did all they could to help and protect themselves and their properties, continually dousing the land with water all around them to create a dampened perimeter and packing up in case of evacuation. Fire is such a scary thing though as it can change direction so quickly. The wind can whip up and turn what was a small-scale fire into a raging inferno, and land that has been dampened down can re-ignite so quickly. The Europe-wide heatwave that we were experiencing at the time also did not help matters as the mercury went above 45 degrees Celsius.

Fóia and Monchique were a terrible reminder of the fragility of our land here, after such a long dry hot summer it can take so little for a fire to start, with devastating consequences. We sat on our balcony on that Saturday night watching from a distance in horror as the flames spread throughout the area; and with several seats to the fires, and no air support able to fly at night, the flames could be seen from miles away. We had friends in Alferce that were evacuated; our friends from Fóia came and stayed with us for several days, and all over the region we heard stories of evacuation, and tragedy.

We were 40 kilometres away from Fóia and yet our garden was covered in a layer of ash the following morning, the air was acrid, and it was quite hard to breathe. Apparently, at its height, the fires could even be seen from the International Space Station.

Once the fires had been extinguished the landscape was left horribly charred and burnt. It will take so long to recover, and for many people life may never quite go back to normal again. It was very strange driving around the Alferce and Monchique area afterwards, so many of the trees and shrubland were destroyed in the blaze, wildlife was scattered, and homes destroyed. As we drove through the main roads we could see the landscape which almost seemed to belong in a movie rather than real life, with burnt-out cars still sat by the side of the road, homes burnt with roofs missing; and the trees that remained were standing silently along the road.

We have kept the information leaflet safely in a drawer, hoping that we will never need to use the advice inside for ourselves, and every summer we hope that the Fóia fires are not repeated anywhere again.

---

1. Safe Communities Portugal (2018). *Safe Village – Safe People*. Accessed 1st March 2020 through their website https://www.safecommunitiesportugal.com/rural-fire-prevention/

28

Healthcare

"Ooh I couldn't live abroad – what about healthcare?!"

We have heard that said to us so many times before, and people often quote the need for having private healthcare insurance as a pre-requisite for being able to live here in Portugal, something which we have never had. We are just regular people on the normal state healthcare system here as residents although I have never actually had to use my *'Documento de Identificação do Utente do SNS'* (health number registration certificate) before ... until recently!

After a late night walk with our little dog on Sunday night, and having a shocking experience with two feral cats attacking us, my leg certainly came off worse with a series of nasty scratches and bites, and it was obvious that at the very least I knew that I would need a tetanus shot.

So I went off to our local Centro de Saúde (health centre) in Lagoa at lunchtime on a Monday with no idea how the system worked, but I was armed with a Google translation of 'I've been bitten by a wild cat.' (*'Mordido por um gato selvagem'* – that seemed to work fine in case you ever need it) and I had a great chewed leg to prove it!

The man at the counter was very helpful and marched me off to the ubiquitous ticket machine and handed me a ticket ... and told me to go and sit in the waiting room and wait for my number to be called. 45 minutes later I was called back to the same man at the same counter. He checked my Utente number on the computer; I duly paid him 4.50 euros and I was given a printed sheet of paper with an appointment to come back at 5.30 p.m. that same day.

I know what you are thinking ... this is the Portuguese system at its finest ... why couldn't I just go up to the man at the counter when I arrived, pay my money and get an appointment ... why did I have to sit for 45 minutes waiting with everyone else in turn to do the same thing ... but this is the way it is; you just must accept some things are done 'a certain way'!

So I returned at 5.30 p.m. and took another seat in the same waiting room expecting to make myself comfortable again. My name was called literally one minute later, and I was straight in to see a very charming and lovely female doctor. Within 10 minutes I had had a tetanus injection, and I left armed with a prescription for antibiotics and advice on keeping my wounds clean ... all for the original 4.50 euros I had paid earlier. I was genuinely amazed that I did not have to pay extra for the tetanus shot.

Off to the chemists I went, and the second shock of the day was the price of my prescription for the antibiotics as they cost me the grand total of 3.57 euros which is quite frankly amazing. Friends on Facebook couldn't believe the low cost of all this, or the fact that I was given an appointment to see a doctor the same afternoon. Perhaps the UK system could learn a few tricks from Portugal.

And for the record a little bottle of something called Betadine is brilliant stuff! It's Povidone-iodine (PVP-I), also known as iodopovidone, and it is an antiseptic you can buy over the counter at the chemists. The iodine in it also stains your skin a fabulous shade of brown which even a local fisherman in the village recognised when I walked past him the next morning, as he gave me a big thumbs-up and shouted,

"Oh Betadine – muito bom!" ("Oh Betadine – very good!")

They do a red bottle too called 'Espuma' which is great for cleaning wounds.

Unlike in the UK, the Portuguese Health System isn't completely free even for Portuguese citizens. Nominal charges are payable by everyone, for tests, GP visits and other procedures; although if my experience is any indication of the pricing structure, it is by no means out of the range of most of the population.

I have to say that I was very impressed with the simple set up and how efficiently and kindly I was dealt with by everyone at the health centre.

Somehow paying our taxes and being legal isn't such a bad thing after all.

✿ಐ✿ҩ✿

For those of you that are interested in finding out more information, historically the fact that if you are a foreigner (EU and non-EU) with residency or a residence permit and/or a work visa this should be sufficient for you to register and gain your Utente Health Care user card/number; although in practice we have heard lots of stories of people needing to produce Social Security registration details before gaining a Utente number now.

The confusion seems to arise from the fact that if you are of legal retirement age and from the UK, you can get an S1 form from the UK that does entitle you to register with the Portuguese system. If, however, you have retired early or are of working age, lots of health centres are now saying that you will only be able to get cover if you have a job in Portugal or become self-employed (and therefore begin to contribute to Portugal's social security system). This does seem to vary depending upon which health centre you register with, and where you are from, and is not strictly true as all residents are entitled to access the national health system regardless of work status. As is often the case, it depends on where you go and who you ask.

If however you plan to apply for residency, and you are not

eligible for Portuguese social healthcare, you will be required to provide proof of private health insurance coverage.

Portugal has a comprehensive system of hospitals and health centres covering every town and village. You might not have to travel very far, but you might have to wait for an appointment at the health centre if your request is not urgent. Larger towns and cities seem to cope well with bookings, but smaller places may only have health centre coverage on one day of the week.

We have discovered however that for most health centres, if you are not feeling well, they run a simple 'triage' style system. You turn up first thing in the morning and depending on how busy they are and how ill you are, you are likely to be given an appointment that same day. You may be asked to wait until there is a gap, or given a time to return, but you have a good chance of seeing a doctor the same day. This certainly eases the pressure on the emergency hospital departments.

Where the system does seem to slow down to a grinding halt is when you require an appointment with a specialist. Stories of people waiting up to two years for an appointment are sadly not that unusual. Staff shortages certainly add to this problem, and which is where the private sector often comes to the rescue.

If you have a Portuguese Utente number, then you can also receive discounted or even free medication, depending on the medication and illness it pertains to. If you don't have a number, you will have to pay full price for your prescription medicine. Many medicines however are available over the counter in Portugal, whereas in other countries you might have to have a prescription. It's worth checking, as I have been surprised at how much the local pharmacy can offer for sale over the counter. It is also worth noting that the pharmacy is the only place that you can purchase medicines here, unlike in the UK where your local supermarket can sell many painkillers and other items directly off the shelf. If you want ibuprofen here, you will have to buy it at the pharmacy; there are no 79 pence cheap packets of pain killers here I'm afraid.

✧ଛ✧୪✧

There are no cheap prescription glasses out here either. We know of lots of people that catch a cheap flight back to the UK and have their eyes tested, wait an hour or maybe 24 hours, collect their new glasses and return to Faro airport, having spent less money in total on their trip and new glasses than they would if they had gone to an opticians locally.

Other people have an eye test locally then use the resulting information to order glasses online. That might work if you have a basic prescription, but if you are like Dave and need special varifocals that require fitting, then the postal route is not an option. Sadly as we discovered not all opticians are the same.

We initially went to a local opticians and Dave had an appointment booked for 4 p.m. He arrived five minutes early to be told that the optician had 'gone for coffee' and would be back soon. Twenty-five minutes later he strolled in. It was not the best start. The eye test was free in that it would be offset against the cost of the purchase of a pair of glasses, but Dave thought it was a very basic test. Nevertheless we went back a week later for the results and to select some new glasses; but the receptionist informed us that she could not find his results. They had been re-organising the office area and she asked if we could return a week later when she assured us that she would have his eye test results ready.

We went back on two more occasions and on the third attempt the receptionist handed us a hand-written test card that had one of Dave's eyes registered as +5.5 and the other as +3.75. This was not what Dave was expecting, and I did joke with him about how poor his eyesight must have deteriorated to have scores like that, which were much worse than his last test a few years previously. We decided to try another optician, concluding that they must have lost Dave's results and just written down some numbers at random to keep us happy.

On a recommendation we then went to a more modern opticians in Lagos and this time we struck gold. They were helpful, efficient, had state-of-the-art equipment and were very thorough indeed. The results were also far closer to what we were expecting! They even created a pair of reading glasses specifically set to the correct distance for Dave's computer work. They were not cheap, but they were worth it. They even let Kat the dog into the reception area, and she had great fun snuffling around and even tried on a pair of glasses herself!

Dental costs are not covered under the Portuguese health system, but you can get some dental costs covered with private health insurance providers. There are dentists in most towns across the Algarve, and we have been delighted with the dentist we have found and signed up with who is local to us here. She is polite, efficient, reassuringly nice and reasonably priced. We were expecting a bit of a shock with the bill the first time we visited her, as we had not been for some time. Two check-ups, cleaning and one filling - all for 125 euros.

And there was no language barrier to worry about as she speaks five languages fluently. Including English ... unlike all the staff in our local pharmacy as you will discover below.

❀ﾟ☆☆☆

As usual what started out as a simple request from Dave turned into one of my finest 'oh dear' moments. He was travelling away, had eaten something that had not agreed with him, and decided that he needed some Imodium tablets 'just in case'. It's the stuff you take to stop you going if you get my drift.

So we pull up outside the pharmacy, and he decides that I am the best person to go in and buy some.

"Go on," he said, "your Portuguese is better than mine."

Well, that might be the case, but I'm by no means fluent, and technical words like diarrhoea are difficult enough to spell in English, let alone pronounce in Portuguese.

"Oh ok," I said, "I'll go in - wish me luck."

'How hard can it be?' I thought to myself, they are bound to speak some English, and I can always resort to sign language if I get stuck.

Well, they didn't speak any English at all, so I reverted to my best Portuguese. I was careful to stress quickly that this was for my husband of course, not for me. I doubt they believed me. I valiantly tried to explain what I needed, but it was obvious neither member of staff behind the counter had got a clue what I was asking for, and they just stared at me in a bemused way.

Oh dear, here goes with the mime then I thought. Well I had better put my acting career on hold, as when I had finished valiantly trying to show what I needed the tablets for, they brought out a bottle of some pink-coloured liquid to show me. Have you ever tried to mime having 'the runs' to put it politely? Well I will never try to again.

In desperation at the end, I said to them (in Portuguese),

"No, it is not a liquid, they are tablets. In English we call it Imodium. I do not know what you call it in Portuguese, sorry."

"Oh", came the reply "We call it Imodium too."

I'm sure I saw the hint of a smirk as the lady said this, and I am quite sure that they knew what I wanted all along!

I managed my revenge on Dave quite unwittingly, however, not long after my infamous Imodium moment. We do get bothered by mosquitoes out here in the summer months, and the blighters seem to particularly enjoy feasting on Dave. I have teased him before that as he is rather lacking in the hirsute department on the top of his head, and what little he does have left is strimmed mercilessly (by me!) they have a nice landing pad to aim for. Or perhaps he just has tasty blood; either way he is the perfect person to stand next to in the evening as they tend to bypass me completely in their excitement to reach Dave.

I do spray some repellent on though, just in case, and favour a spray called 'Skin So Soft' by Avon. It has no nasty chemicals and a pleasant aroma that even Dave doesn't mind. We were meeting friends and intending to sit outside to eat dinner, so out came a new bottle of spray, which I then placed in my handbag once we had doused ourselves.

All went well until the evening grew dark, and I glanced over at

Dave and noticed that his head was glowing and very sparkly. I checked my forearms, and yes, they were all shiny and glittery too. I surreptitiously pulled the bottle of spray from my bag and had a closer look at the blurb on the front. The label proclaimed: 'Contains Glitter. Add Sparkle to your Evening'. Oh dear! Of course I told him; and of course we laughed. A lot.

29

Entertainment

We have never been huge fans of watching television, I think the last time we watched Eastenders, Dirty Den and Angie had leading roles in the soap world, but when we moved out here we did bring a Freesat box with us and had a giant paella dish of a satellite installed on the roof of the house. It was entertaining for about a week, and then we realised that walking on a beach was more fun that watching breakfast TV, and that sitting outside in the evening sunshine and enjoying a relaxed and leisurely meal was infinitely more enjoyable than sitting in front of the TV in the lounge.

However there came a day that the UK changed their satellite beam from what has theatrically been described as the 'old beam' which was like all the stage lights being switched on and illuminating the whole cast on the stage of the theatre, and which covered most of western Europe; to the 'new beam' which is the equivalent of a single beam on the centre of the stage only picking out the lead actor. The consequence was that it left all of Europe firmly in the dark - including Portugal.

The outpouring of grief from the expat UK community was tangible with comments like,

"What will we do without our [technically illegal] British TV now that it has gone?"

Well, we had a few suggestions, but we decided to keep quiet! Then began the fun of watching the sudden rise of lots of 'unofficial companies offering unofficial products' all promising to be able to 'legally stream UK TV [sort of] illegally'. These 'products' however had a nasty habit of failing the viewer at critical moments - like five minutes before the end of the European Cup Final in football, or the grand final of Strictly at Christmas. Oh dear!

We have ventured to the cinema quite a few times, many of the big movies are shown here almost concurrent with being shown in the UK, and apart from children's movies that are almost always dubbed into Portuguese; you can usually select to watch a movie in English.

Many of the cinemas are in large shopping centres and have multiple theatres showing different movies. They are often not well used though, if our experience watching the opening night of the latest James Bond movie recently was anything to go by, as there were only 12 people including us sat in the cinema. It does make it feel like you are sat in your own private cinema though. We have been the only two people sat in the cinema one afternoon and had the whole screening to ourselves.

One thing that takes some getting used to at the cinema is the random intermission break that will occur. You have no warning that it is about to happen; the only thing we can think is that they literally stop the movie at the half-way point. That might be in the middle of a sentence, or a car chase, or a defining moment in the plot. Everyone tends to go out and have a toilet break or grab a quick coffee. You also usually have absolutely no idea how long the break is going to be (it is usually about 15 minutes) so you have to hover back in the doorway or sit down in an empty cinema waiting for the plot to resume - which it does again with no warning!

Portuguese TV has never really appealed to us. Every bar, café and restaurant out here have a small, or usually not so small, television, fixed precariously into the top corner of the room. You can blame the 2004 UFA Euro Football Final for that as Portugal hosted the finals and virtually every establishment that serves food had a television installed to watch the football. Being in Portugal when Portugal wins a football competition is quite an experience. The Portuguese love their football and it is quite infectious and easy to be drawn in to watching and celebrating with them. The UEFA 2016 final where Portugal beat France in extra time was a fantastic day here. I have never heard so many car horns blaring for hours after they had lifted the cup.

The only Portuguese television that I watch is the daytime chat show 'Querida Julia' which is on in the background every time that I go to my local hairdressers. It is quite an experience. I think it was the morning that I went for my regular haircut and found myself inexplicably drawn to the TV screen in the corner in both sheer horror and fascination as the theme for the entire morning's programme was - how can I put this politely? - topiary for 'down there'. I kid you not!

The sight of a young girl's 'lady garden' which had been neatly trimmed and died bright green, complete with a tattoo and arrow proudly proclaiming 'do not sit on the grass' was just too much to cope with at 10.30 a.m. Captive audience that I was whilst my hair was being lopped off and deftly styled, and even with my limited grasp of Portuguese, I managed to get the gist of what Julia and her trio of sofa guides were chatting about. It caused much hilarity in the hairdressers though.

Maybe it is just the times of day that we are generally out and about, but the Portuguese television that we tend to catch seems to be American-style soap operas. They usually consist of a good-looking man racing off in a sports car, leaving behind a disgruntled woman with long hair who is angry about something, and ends up flicking her hair around in a most dismissive manner whilst folding her arms in 'that way' that suggests that the sports car man really shouldn't have said what he did before he drove off. Or there is a family that always sit around a kitchen table that look like they have come straight from the 1970's complete with Formica table and chairs and a fabulous on-set wardrobe that consists of an interesting collection of hand-knitted jumpers. That is of course if you manage to find a programme between the interminably long intermission advert breaks that can easily last twenty minutes.

Perhaps I am being a little unfair, I am sure that there are some good Portuguese documentary programmes out there too, but they don't seem to be on the channels that all the cafés and bars tend to show. The news channel RTP is always on in my local café where I stop off every morning whilst walking Kat the dog and seems to be a good source of informative news. Luckily our local café adds the subtitles underneath as well on the news ticker at the bottom of the screen, so I can usually get the gist of what has happened in the world overnight.

I cannot be too rude about the RTP channel as they did feature Dave and I one evening on the national 8 p.m. news! We were interviewed for a whole 2-minute slot in a feature on Brexit and its implications. We discovered later that they had struggled to find a British couple living legally in the Algarve that voted to Remain in the Brexit referendum that were willing to be interviewed for national TV. Step forward an unlikely couple and a cute Spanish water dog (well of course Kat the dog came too and was the star of the show) for their two minutes of TV fame.

What was fascinating after the event was enjoying friends' reactions afterwards - or should I say Portuguese friends' reactions as we realised that none of our non-Portuguese friends have Portuguese TV or watch Portuguese news, as not one of our non-Portuguese friends even mentioned it! However for several days afterwards wherever we went out, our Portuguese friends, neighbours, and even strangers in the street shouted out to us,

"We saw you on TV!"

I went back to my local hairdressers again just in time for our brief TV appearance to have been watched and commented upon. There isn't much that is missed there, it is a fabulous local place that only charge me 9 euros for a haircut, and it is almost worth paying that for the entertainment value alone. It is the setting for all the local gossip in the town to be shared, and I discovered after a few haircuts there, that at least half the women sat in the chairs are not waiting to have their hair done at all, they are just there to find out the latest snippets of news and information.

Sadly for me the speed at which most of them gossip is alarmingly fast, and I am regularly left bemused by the snatches of conversation that I try to listen to. Usually I can manage to understand about one word in ten that flies past me, so I can usually work out, for example, that they are talking about someone's grandmother, and a cat and something about a tree being cut down. I happily settle back and make up the rest of the story in my head; doubtless it will be less savoury than the actual news they are retelling, but it keeps me amused. And there is always the topiary to ponder upon as well!

Most of the entertainment in the village is subtle and enjoyable. Only this morning I spent an entertaining twenty minutes talking with the owner of the antique shop in the village and one of the retired fishermen who doesn't speak at all but who uses sign language to great effect. What is lovely is that so many of the other local men of his age have learnt to communicate with him too via sign language. He does a great impression of me striding along walking Kat the dog every morning with my arms swinging along ... he also adds a great big smile for effect too, so I guess I must look happy as I walk each morning!

Today we had a great three-way conversation with me speaking basic Portuguese, the fisherman signing away and the antique shop man translating both ways. I learnt more about the locals walking past us in twenty minutes through sign language than I ever would talking to someone, although I am hoping that the hand signals he demonstrated when he pointed out his retired schoolteacher (who he proudly told me was 93) correlated to the fact that she still takes in ironing and has nothing to do with working in the solitary lap-dancing establishment in the village!

The antique shop man always gives me a wry smile and a thumbs-up when he sees me ... another sad example of my poor grasp of the Portuguese language. He has a very nice little yellow canary that sits chirping away at passers-by all day outside his shop, and Kat the dog always stops for a look and a sniff at the cage as we go past.

I saw him one day at our café, and I know the Portuguese word for bird is *pássaro* ... for some reason my brain went into a different category and I managed to ask him,

"How is your duck today?" (saying the word *pato* instead of *pássaro*), to which he looked rather bemused and replied,

"I do not have a duck."

Still vainly limping on in Portuguese I made it even worse by saying,

"Yes you do, it is the yellow bird in the cage outside your shop."

Don't ask how I managed to put all that together in Portuguese but failed to get the name of the bird right.

"Ah!" he said in English, "you mean my bird ..." and then said in Portuguese,

"*meu canário.*" (the canary)

Yes that will be the one ... another Portuguese word that sounds just like the English one ... which reminds me of the day I asked someone,

"What is the Portuguese for picnic?"

The reply, of course, was,

"*Picnic.*"

30

Beaches to Explore

T he Algarve is known for its stunning coastline and beautiful beaches and we have enjoyed exploring so many of them over the years. We also enjoy sneaking our way up onto the West Coast around Aljezur as well so trying to choose just a few of our favourite beaches in the Algarve to share for this book was always going to be difficult.

The Algarve has been voted Europe's top beach destination and it's not hard to see why. Whether you are a family, sunbather, surfer, walker or sunset lover, there will be a beach for you somewhere out here, as you have over 150 beaches to choose from.

These are just some of our favourites…

Praia do Amado

Wild, unspoilt and great for surfing! This is a wonderful beach to get away from it all and has soft sand and huge big skies. There is also an international surf school here. The beach is on the west coast near Carrapateira. It is about 1 kilometre of sand in total and at low tide you can walk through several bays.

The beach is surrounded by an amazing set of cliffs. The artist in me of course loves the beautiful range of colours from sand and ochre, to bright red and pink. The rock formations on the west coast are truly stunning and Amado is one of the best examples of this wonder of nature.

The beach is an extremely popular spot for surfers, some say it even has the perfect conditions for surfing. They hold international surfing competitions here so it must be good. The waves in the winter can be amazing, certainly not suitable for beginners ... although wonderful to watch.

It is a beach that never gets crowded even in summer, the sand is soft and perfect for walking along the water's edge.

There are also some fabulous walking trails to discover on the cliffs overhead, with the most stunning views. You can walk from Amado beach all the way to Bordeira beach which will give you lots of opportunity to enjoy the cliff-top views and the enormous big skies overhead.

Bordeira

This is a wide and open large beach, with sand dunes and lots to explore. You are almost guaranteed to find some space on this beach even in the summer. Follow the signs for Carrapateira, then Bordeira, and then park up and walk along a wooden boardwalk to reach the beach and look out for the surfer's beach hut too, it's a real feature of the beach.

Bordeira is often deserted, and in the winter, you can often have the beach all to yourself. We love this time of year, exploring the sand dunes and the tiny river with its migrating water birds.

Praia de Molhe and Praia Grande, Ferragudo

Molhe is a small beach with a big heart. It is one of the most stunning small beaches from which to capture an amazing sunset. It is on the way to Carvoeiro from Ferragudo and has a long man-made pier with a lighthouse on the end. It is a favourite spot for a late afternoon promenade, it is not busy or touristy, and has a small beach with soft sand in a protected bay.

Around the corner from Molhe and situated on the eastern shores of the mouth of the River Arade, just across the water from Praia da Rocha and Portimão, is the wide sandy stretch of Praia Grande. It translates as 'big beach' and is over a mile long. It has wonderful soft sand, a protected bay, and the beachside cafés and boats moored in the harbour in the summer months give this a real holiday tourist feel. Most holidaymakers only walk from the end of the wooden boardwalk to the nearest sun lounger though, so if you are willing to walk a little way further, you can find yourself an unoccupied stretch of beach.

Praia Grande is Ferragudo's main beach and as such has plenty of facilities such as cafés and shops. It is a popular spot and can become quite busy in the summer months. It is a great beach for families, with water sports, a lifeguard and a relatively safe bay for swimming.

The northern end of the beach has the imposing feature of the 16th century fort of São João do Arade. Originally built to defend the coast from pirates, the fort is now privately owned and has been sympathetically restored.

It is also our local beach and Kat and I can be seen there most mornings in winter walking the soft sand, skipping the gentle waves and chasing the pigeons out from under the castle walls!

Praia da Marinha

This is the beach that has the views that are so iconic to the Algarve with its crumbling cliffs, hidden coves and incredible arches of rock reaching out into the sea. Marinha is one of several beaches east of Carvoeiro, near Armação de Pêra. Access to the beach is via some steep steps or you can enjoy the views from the cliff-top walks above.

It is a large cove with lots of caves and rock pools to explore. It is a relatively small beach with a lack of tourist facilities or cafés, which is probably why we like it so much. It is, however, the colour of the sea and sky against the majestic limestone cliffs that sets this beach apart and ensures that it is a well-photographed and promoted beach.

Monte Clérigo

Back to the west coast for this beach which is near Aljezur. This is a delightful beach with wide open sand, good body-boarding waves, and the most stunning small black rocks that are washed up on the beach.

The Algarve's west coast has an unspoilt feel with wide sandy beaches bracing themselves against the full force of the Atlantic Ocean. This beach is in the Vicentina Coast Natural Park, which is an area of outstanding natural beauty, and is Dave's absolute favourite beach anywhere in the world.

The beach has golden sand with cliffs to either end, it is the perfect beach to walk along at low tide. Kat the dog loves to explore the rock pools to the left of the main beach, and Dave is always busy with his camera capturing the waves, big skies and pretty village in the background. There are a couple of cafés, a restaurant, toilets and lifeguards in the summer. But it is in winter when this beach comes to life, with the Atlantic swells and bracing fresh air.

A word of warning though … the waves here can really catch you out! We were there on a lovely February afternoon walking along a relatively low tide enjoying the view. Our first mistake was to turn our backs to the sea as Dave wanted to capture a shot of the village nestling on the cliff side. Our second mistake was to miss the roar of a wave approaching … five seconds later the wave had passed us, and we were soaking wet from the top of our legs down to our feet. In February. Whilst wearing jeans.

We scampered over to the rocks and tried to dry out. It was impossible. We took off our jeans, hurray for long jumpers (!) and draped our wet jeans on a rock in the sun and proceeded to wait. We made up a game: who can throw their handful of little stones closest to the big stone we had stood up in the ground. All was fine until we heard a family approaching. They were French, they stood and pointed, talked rapidly then stared at us. I wished my

French was better, but I guessed the gist of what they were saying was,

"Why are those silly people over there throwing rocks and not wearing their trousers?"

To round it off, our jeans were still soaking wet two hours later; we drove home sat on towels squelching water and raced upstairs to shower and change when we finally got home. The moral of the story? ... Look behind you!

Armação de Pêra and Salgados

This is a long expanse of wide sand, with beach bars and fishermen mending their nets. As a beach, this seems to sum up the two extremes of Portuguese beaches as it is a working fisherman's beach and a great tourist sunbathing site.

About a kilometre east of Armação de Pêra is Praia dos Salgados. It is part of one long expanse of beach that stretches for miles, but there are named sections along the way, even if no-one quite knows where one ends and the next begins.

Unlike the coast further east, which is backed by cliffs and rocks, Praia dos Salgados has low sand dunes. These are covered over by wooden boardwalks to protect the local environment and nature, and the walkways are great for a leisurely and easy walk.

Beyond the sand dunes lies the Salgados Lagoon, which is one of our favourite afternoon strolls. Many migrating birds use the wetlands as a stopover and nest among the reeds. If you are lucky you can also spot herons and flamingos here and if you lean over the bridge on the walkway you can watch the turtles swimming in the water.

Evaristo beach

This beach near Albufeira has a lovely restaurant overlooking the beach and is a great location for exploring and searching the many rock pools. Disabled access is good with a boardwalk running down to and along the beach.

It has good facilities and even the chance of some celebrity-spotting too. The restaurant of the same name is right on the beach and has an enviable menu of fish and seafood, and attracts famous and wealthy people, although you can always just order a drink and sit here watching the sunset.

Galé Beach

This is a wide and sheltered beach, with amazing rock formations at the eastern end to explore. This is one for a long leisurely walk along after lunch and another great place to watch the sun set.

The beach is easily accessible, with ramps to help you across the dunes. This is a long five kilometre stretch of sand with beachside restaurants and cafés. You can hire a sun lounger, explore the fossil-laden rocks or swim in safe water that is patrolled by lifeguards in the summer.

Praia dos Três Irmãos

This is actually just the eastern end of Alvor beach and is named after the three jutting rocks or 'three brothers' that extend into the sea, creating a stunning backdrop and a beautiful beach location to relax and enjoy. With golden sand, and smaller coves to explore at low tide, this is a real treasure. There are also several good beach restaurants and cafés here too.

You can walk at low tide along the adjoining sandy bays, that each have their own rock arches, caves and limestone cliffs to enjoy. One of these bays, Prainha, meaning 'little beach', is a favourite of ours at low tide.

There are plenty of facilities on the beach including toilets, there is good disabled access, excellent restaurants and a summer lifeguard service.

Amoreira beach

Back to Aljezur on the west coast for this beach which is a real hidden treasure, it has such an unspoilt and magical feel to it. Drive through Aljezur, then turn left at the sports centre and then it's a long drive down a windy and bumpy track, but it is well worth it once you arrive at the simple car park at the end and see the view ahead of you.

The beach has beautiful soft sand, backed by sand dunes, and has the most stunning rock formations and a river beach lagoon at low tide. There is also a lovely restaurant overlooking the beach ... perfection!

Benagil

East of Carvoeiro is the little fishing village of Benagil. This is still a working fishing village with boats pulled up on the beach at the bottom of the slipway. The beach is unspoilt, although parking is difficult as there is no car park, just on-road parking.

The limestone cliffs here are stunningly beautiful, and colourful carved arches form an amazing backdrop to this little beach. One of the most iconic and photographed structures must be the Algar de Benagil nearby, which is a cathedral-like cave with arched entrances and a small beach inside. Many people travel by boat trip to set foot inside this cavernous structure; but beware the tide though as you get out of the boat as you can easily be tipped into the water!

Praia do Barril

Travelling much further east now the beach of Praia do Barril is located on the Ilha de Tavira, just west of the town of Tavira. This beach has a huge stretch of white sand and you are almost guaranteed some peace and quiet on this beach. Just a warning though that the western end of the beach is designated as an official nudist beach.

The beach is most famous for the Anchor Graveyard or

'Cemitério das Âncoras' which can be found amongst the dunes. The sight of hundreds of rusting and rotting anchors all lined up in rows is quite something. The area used to be a major tuna fishing area, and the anchors were used to tie the tuna nets in place. Sadly with the decline of the industry the anchors were left to rot and are still there to this day.

Ilha da Cultura

The Ilha da Cultura is a small and sandy island located behind the Ria Formosa nature reserve off the coast of Faro. It is only accessible by a ferry from Faro and offers over two kilometres of soft sand with gentle sand dunes and is a peaceful retreat from the world. Pack a picnic and make a day trip here, you will not be disappointed.

There are so many gorgeous places to enjoy along this stunning coastline. These are just a selection of our favourites, and we still have so many places that we have not visited or explored yet. How lucky we are to live in such a beautiful part of the world.

31

Wonderful Walks

The Algarve is not just all beaches and holidaymakers. There are so many beautiful and unspoilt areas just waiting to be explored away from the main tourist areas. The most well recognised must be the official network of footpaths called the Via Algarviana which is all neatly signed and arranged across the Algarve. The route starts in Alcoutim, near the Guadiana River and extends across the Algarve region to Cabo de São Vicente. The route traces over an old trail used by pilgrims to reach the Promontory of Sagres, which was a significant location dating from the age of the Descobrimentos (Portuguese Discoveries).

This is a real walk into nature, meandering through small villages, and wandering alongside riverbanks and streams. The route takes you up to Monchique, with its stunning panoramic views from Picota and Fóia, and then through pine forests and rural countryside. You finish at the most southerly point in Europe at Sagres and Cabo de São Vicente, in the Costa Vicentina Natural Park, with its beautiful natural coastline. The route stretches for almost 300 kilometres, and is broken down into sections, with suitable tourist accommodation recommended all along the route.

Some of our favourite walks however are a bit shorter than that! Having a dog means that you get to explore so much more of the area in which you live, and Kat the dog likes nothing better than a good snuffle and explore, which gives me lots of time to enjoy the views and tranquillity of so much of this beautiful place we call home.

One of our nearby favourites must be the Parque Municipal das Fontes (the Municipal Park of the Springs), which is locally and more commonly known as the Fontes de Estômbar (The Estômbar Springs). It is a park situated on the left bank of the estuary of the Arade River, north of the town of Estômbar, in the Lagoa Municipality.

The park, formally created in 1989, consists of about 18 hectares and is an important ecosystem site for nature. The park has a restored watermill, a reconstructed traditional Algarve house, an open-air amphitheatre, picnic area, river walk, and an area for physical fitness and exercise.

The site is also historically and culturally important since vestiges of human activities dating back to pre-historic times have been found there. A watermill is documented in the archive book entitled the 'Livro do Almoxarifado de Silves' (from the 15th century), which records a 'site of springs where [a man called] Vicente Pirez has a mill.'

Beside the remains of this mill, the pools created by the springs are also used for bathing in the summer months although it's not for the faint hearted as the water is freezing cold. The water is so clear and fresh, you can see the pebbles on the bottom, and it is a great spot to roll up your trouser legs and dangle your feet in the water.

It is such a peaceful and quiet place ... we don't want too many people to find it!

The first thing that we always do after we have parked is follow the path that leads down to the water and take the beautiful woodland path that follows the line of the river Arade. It is a fabulous place to walk Kat too as there are lots of rabbit trails to sniff! You can walk much further than you think ... all the way to a little wooden jetty where you can enjoy spectacular views across the river.

The wildlife and flowers are wonderful at any time of year, including some rare and delicate plants hidden in the grass, and there are lots of wild orchids. The birds are often a bit more hidden but if you are patient you can catch some fantastic sights including cormorants sat patiently fishing.

The park has a gentle sense of conservation and nature combining well with man-made facilities. The site has a well-signed exercise route scattered amongst the trees and paths, although the main feature of the park for many is the picnic area. This can get extremely busy in the summer at weekends, full of local people sat in large groups of families and friends, all enjoying a relaxing picnic whilst enjoying the view over the lake. The site also has built in barbecues, you can just bring your own charcoal or share with others.

There are toilets on site and plenty of rubbish and recycling bins, and we've never seen any rubbish left lying around, as everyone seems very respectful of the beauty of the area. It is all very well maintained, and even has a security guard during opening times.

We keep meaning to go to one of the annual events that the site hosts, they have a Jazz Festival each summer, and in the autumn there is an annual festival that promotes the didgeridoo and the Australian Aboriginal culture in Portugal, when the site is transformed into an alternative festival ground.

It's great to see the venue is well used, however the real enjoyment for us comes with simply arriving there on a quiet afternoon and going for a walk. So if you go there enjoy the peace and tranquillity, and the beautiful scenery … and watch out for a little Spanish water dog scuttling along sniffing out the rabbits!

○⁊○⊙○

Another lovely area to explore are the hills surrounding Monchique, and we were lucky enough to be invited to experience something different one spring day ... a chance to explore a part of the Algarve which is missing on most tourist maps.

Our house has a fabulous view of the Monchique mountain range, and the highest point on the Algarve which is Fóia but we had never had the chance to explore the mountain walks around the area; so when Fiona from the website 'My Destination Algarve' invited us to join her on a walk and lunch we jumped at the chance! We were also introduced to an absolute gem of a restaurant tucked between Monchique and Fóia, as the then owner of 'Jardim das Oliveiras' (Garden of the Olive Trees) António Baiona was our host for the day, and he had lots of surprises for us on our day out exploring and eating our way around the mountain. (Sadly due to ill health the restaurant has now changed hands, it is still a great place to eat, but António has since retired).

We started by meeting at the restaurant for breakfast and we were absolutely spoilt with a traditional 'local farmer's breakfast' ... complete with large flat churros served with cinnamon and sugar; a toasted eggy bread called *fatias douradas*; and a local black pudding, which was delicious. All washed down with a large coffee and we were ready for our walk. Well I think what I really needed was a lie-down and a nap for a while, we had eaten so much food!

The restaurant is situated in a beautiful spot, with views over the valley below, and António was rightly proud of all that he had achieved at his restaurant in the fifteen years that he owned it. He also has great links with the local people, and we were introduced to our guide for the morning, Filipe, who was a local man with an amazing knowledge of the local area.

We were dropped off at the top of Fóia, with its spectacular views across the countryside. On a clear day you can literally see for miles around. We were quite pleased with the arrangements which were described to us as follows,

"We'll drop you off at the top and then you can walk back down the mountainside and meet back at the restaurant for lunch!"

I couldn't imagine being able to eat another thing at that moment; but figured that by the time we had done all that walking in the fresh air, we'd be hungry again.

It soon became apparent that Filipe knew the land like his own back garden, and we were soon diverting off the tourist road onto smaller tracks and trails … all the time heading downwards! It is fair to say that this would not be a route for the faint hearted or a terribly unfit person, but it was worth all the effort and rock hopping to enjoy the most amazing views and scenery.

We stopped several times just to enjoy the view and take photos, and Filipe told us stories about almost every ruin that we passed. The area was obviously once a thriving farming community, with stories of families helping each other with threshing, hay stored in barns, and cattle and sheep roaming the landscape. We passed eerily deserted and ramshackle old buildings, where you could still see where the animals would have been housed, and where the fresh springs of water and dried stream beds criss-crossed the hillside.

The landscape is full of tiered and walled sections making the best use of the land, and we saw a fantastic selection of majestic trees; eucalyptus woods; and the tiniest prettiest little orange and white flowers that littered the grass. Filipe pointed out one flower called the Adelfa plant, which he told us was highly poisonous if eaten, and only found in three places in the world. It was fascinating to go home and look this one up later, and I'm glad we left it well alone.

The sights and smells were wonderful, with the cleanest fresh air, and the heady scent of eucalyptus and blossom to accompany us all the way.

At one point we stopped at a little house nestled into the hillside, and Filipe assured us he knew the owner, so we explored and re-filled our water bottles from the freshwater spring beside the house. It was of course *vende-se* (for sale) as so many little houses are across the region. It was a tempting thought!

We loved the owner's home-made bird-scarer too, which comprised of a line strung with empty green wine bottles, and it made a very pleasant sound as the wind caught the bottles, and presumably kept the birds at bay.

Having a local person to guide us was a real treat … we felt that we saw the 'real' Monchique, and met some fascinating people, including a quick trip to a local Medronho distillers, which was a tiny little local building tucked away and which we would never had realised was there if it wasn't for Filipe. We of course had to sample a little 'fire water' and that certainly helped us to complete the last hour of the walk. They also made their own local honey too so now we know where to go to buy some fresh, local and clear honey all made from local bees.

Next stop on the way down was a real hidden gem. I have no idea how we would get to it again though, but António and his driver met us with his mini-bus and dropped us off at a local tourist spot. It was a beautifully restored old water mill called 'O Moinho de Água do Poucochinho'. Sadly the 'key' had gone to lunch (!) so we couldn't explore inside but there's always next time if we can find it again!

And then it was a quick drive back to the restaurant and time for our lunch, and what a lunch, it was one of the nicest meals we have ever eaten anywhere on the Algarve.

António prided himself on providing traditional local Portuguese food. He described how the families of previous generations would have all cooked their food in an oak-smoked wood oven, and that many people do not have these anymore, and so by cooking in this traditional way, he delighted in reminding people of the flavours and food of their childhood and history. The resulting food was superb with rich flavours, beautiful presentation, and was a delight to enjoy.

We started with a selection of starters, including chirozo sausage, fried mushrooms, and prawn cocktail with mango, served with the freshest bread. This is the simple tasty fare the Portuguese are renowned for.

The main course was a first for us as we tried wild boar in a delicious stew. It was so well cooked it just fell apart and melted in the mouth and was perfect paired with a glass of local red wine.

The restaurant itself has a lovely unpretentious feel to it, there are separate smaller rooms for private functions too, and a lovely outdoor eating area, complete with a play area for children. There are even hammocks in the garden if you eat too much and need a rest afterwards!

The real treat though was the guided walk. Having a local person take us 'off the trail' and lead us with stories and a smile across such a beautiful landscape was a brilliant way of finding a different Algarve, and to top it off with such a wonderful lunch really made this the perfect day out.

32

Local History

For a touch of local history you cannot go wrong if you visit Silves, as there is culture and heritage on every corner of this wonderful place; hinting at its affluent and colourful past as the Moorish capital known as Xelb, capital of Al-faghar, which was the province now known as the Algarve.

The origins of the town can be traced back as far as the Roman conquest of the Iberian Peninsula, however it was the occupation in the 8th Century by the Moors which brought a lavish lifestyle to the area. By the 11th century Silves was the capital of the Algarve and the Moors were reputed to have imported lions and other wild animals that roamed freely through the exotic gardens in the centre of the town. It was ruled by the Seville-based Arabic ruler Al-Mu'tamid (Muhammad Ibn Abbad Al Mutamid) who became the governor of Silves and Emir of Seville at the ripe old age of 13.

The area saw many battles between the Christians and Muslims in the 12th and 13th centuries; until Portugal's King Sancho I and the Knights of Santiago captured the city in 1189 with the help of the Anglo-Norman Crusaders. It was recaptured by the Moors in 1191; and was finally re-conquered during the Christian occupation of 1242 to 1249 during the reign of King Afonso III, who also founded the first cathedral, thought to have been built on the site of the former Mosque. With a rich tapestry of history like this, it is no surprise that the area has a fabulous wealth of heritage on show, and it is one of our favourite places to wander around.

Sadly, the earthquake of 1755 caused great damage in the city and nearly all of buildings were destroyed. It is reported that only 20 houses were left standing in the city.

The turret of one of the main City Gates, the *'Torreão da Porta da Cidade'*; is the only one of the four archways to the almedina that remains standing today and it is a very impressive sight, hinting at the fortress-like protection once afforded to the occupants of the city. It is a magnificently tall structure, creating images of biblical-sized enemies and soldiers attacking each other, although it now has a more genteel purpose, housing the municipal library.

Standing underneath the arch you really do feel dwarfed, and if you head up to the entrance of the castle, you will come to the statue of Sancho I of Portugal, known as the Populator; who was the second king of Portugal. The statue is enormous and would fit nicely under the arch. Perhaps the people were all a bit taller back then!

A climb up the narrow and cobbled streets from the arch will lead you to the Cathedral of Silves, which is one of the Algarve's few remaining gothic monuments and an absolute treat. Entrance is only 1 euro. The cathedral was originally built in the 13th century, with 15th and 16th century additions, and post-earthquake 18th century repairs.

The exterior is a wonderful mix of whitewashed walls and red sandstone, and the interior does not fail to delight, with a mixture of Gothic, Medieval and Baroque traditions all sitting comfortably together. There is an immense sense of height and space in the building, with religious music playing quietly in the background. There is an awareness of both the sacred and the human combined, as this feels like a place of worship in the present day as well as an historical record of the past. It is also a very peaceful place, and unusually empty of much of the gold trappings of many local churches.

In direct contrast is the Santa Misericórdia Church which is situated directly opposite the cathedral. My favourite part of this building is the rather magnificent Manueline style door which is set halfway up the outside wall of the building. If you stepped out of it by mistake you would have quite a shock!

The church is originally from the 16th century, and still has a beautifully painted altarpiece of Our Lady of Mercy visible on the walls. The building is now used as an art gallery, although it is often sadly closed.

Up the hill a bit further and you will come to Silves Castle, which is now the best-preserved castle in the Algarve. It is believed to have been situated on top of Roman fortifications from the 4th or 5th century and was built on the site of the 'Palace of the Verandhas', whose construction started around 715 by the Moorish occupants.

It is a most impressive site, with eleven square towers and red sandstone walls which enclose an area of 12,000 metres². Some of the towers have Gothic doorways and there are some small exhibition rooms housing artefacts and displays. There were originally two entrances to the castle grounds; the main gate defended by two towers and a so-called 'traitors-gate'. You can see many areas of excavation, both of historical and archaeological importance, as you walk around the ramparts.

The view from the top is stunning, with panoramic views across the city and surrounding countryside, although the walkways are not for the faint hearted or young. In many places there are no railings and there is quite a drop!

The main central area has a well-tended garden area with trees and seating. There are also two Roman cisterns, the larger one is called *El Moura Encantada* (the enchanted Moura), after a legend that says you can hear a Moorish princess mourning her beloved at the well where he committed suicide. You can view this cistern underground; it has clear Perspex glass walkways over the water, and it is quite eerie. The views across Silves and the neighbouring countryside more than make up for this though, and it is well worth a trip up to the castle - if you don't mind the climb! Watch out if it has been raining, as the combination of worn smooth calçada stones and wet weather can be lethal.

✧℘✧☙✧

For a spooky adventure though you need to travel to Faro and have an osseous experience at the Chapel of Bones church. The church seems to have at least three names: The Carmelite church 'Igreja de Nossa Senhora do Monte do Carmo do Faro' or the 'Igreja do Carmo', or the so-called 'golden' 'Nossa Senhora do Carmo' church. It is situated in the Largo do Carmo square in the Riberinho neighbourhood of Faro, and it is open every day. Admission to the church is free, and the 'Chapel of Bones' visit costs only 1 euro.

The church was started in 1713 and finished in the 19th century. It has a lovely balance to its design from the outside with a bell tower to each side and some impressive steps leading up to the entrance. Inside it has a Baroque altar which is reported to be the best example of gold-leaf woodwork in Portugal, and there is a rich opulence to the interior, with art and statues and gold in abundance. It is certainly a bright contrast to the colder stone interior of Silves cathedral.

But the real delight lies to the right of the main altar where you can buy a ticket for the spooky *Capela dos Ossos* (Chapel of Bones). The chapel was the work of Carmelite monks in 1816 and its construction displaced a cemetery where hundreds of their earlier brethren lay buried. Their human bones were salvaged and recycled into this haunting reminder of our mortality.

The inscription over the door reads 'Stop here and think of the fate that will befall you – 1816', and there are reputed to be approximately 1245 bones covering the walls and ceiling of the chapel.

Macabre? – yes. But also strangely comforting and captivating. The longer you look, the more you see different faces and shapes emerging; the whole chapel and each of the bones have been painstakingly arranged and ordered, and the skulls in particular seem to haunt you and draw you into their history and story.

It's certainly worth a visit if you are in Faro, although stepping out of the cold chapel back into the warm sunlight of the city, and its slightly disarming 21st century hustle and bustle, can be a slight shock to the system.

✿➂✿⊂➂✿

Another of our memorable trips was in the town of Monchique, visiting the 'Convento Nossa Senhora de Desterro' or Our Lady of Exile Convent.

This is a once beautiful, and sadly now derelict, 17th century Franciscan convent situated on a hill overlooking Monchique. We had been intrigued by this old stately building, which is obviously ruined and derelict, on previous visits to the town. You get a great view of it from the wide viewing gallery situated on the opposite side of town, but we had never ventured to walk up there and have a look at it before.

There is quite a climb to explore the convent, and here's the warning – it's a very steep and long climb! It is easy to find if you follow the brown tourist signs from the main square. The signs always make me smile as they look like two old people stooped over and struggling to walk … one of them even has a walking stick. In this case however they seemed to give a fair warning - if you aren't old and stooped when you start this climb you will be when you arrive!

The climb takes you up and out of the main houses, and then into the most picturesque little woodland walk with fantastic views back over Monchique. It is almost British in its woodland feel with shady trees and a windy little path, which is quite rocky and steep in places.

We arrived at the top and initially thought it was all closed off and abandoned. It is certainly an imposing and sadly neglected sight, but you can still get a feel for how majestic and wonderful it would have been when it was in its full splendour:

We were greeted by an old Portuguese gentleman who looked quite astonished to see us and acted as if he hadn't had any visitors for a long while. We had no idea who he was, but he insisted on showing us around, via a little side door that led into a stunning old courtyard. In our broken Portuguese and his enthusiasm, he explained how old the convent was, even drawing the dates in the soil for us to make sure that we knew that it was founded in 1631.

And then he left us to explore. We started to look around and the climb was definitely worth it as we stumbled into old atriums, a chapel, refectory and lots of smaller rooms all now in a ruined state, but still holding their own charm and history.

The courtyard was beautiful and full of chickens, flowering trees and fruit. In the centre was a magnificent old magnolia tree that was supposedly brought over from India by Pêro da Silva, a Viceroy of India, who ordered the convent to be built. This magnolia tree, considered to be the largest in Europe, is over 300 years old. Legend has it that Pêro da Silva is believed to have been buried at the convent, although we didn't see any sign of such a burial plot.

The old refectory still had the remains of what would have once been a stunning tiled centrepiece on the wall depicting Leonardo da Vinci's The Last Supper.

And there are still old tiled crosses visible on the walls that apparently made up part of what was known as the *Via Sacra* (The Sacred Way) which was a religious prayer path within the convent walls.

As we left the old man gave me a flower plucked from the magnolia tree and was effusive in his praise and pride for the old building.

Outside it was sad to see the ruined building decaying and sprayed with graffiti and red painted signs, and we marvelled at how beautiful it would have been when it was first built.

We thought that was the last we would hear about the convent, and then only a couple of weeks later we were amazed to read an article in the local English-speaking Portugal Resident newspaper with the headline:

'Petition to save abandoned national monument.'

The article continued to describe the building as follows:

"Monchique's 17th century Franciscan Convent ... which has been abandoned by the authorities and left to be squatted by a family who have lived there for 36 years. The Algarve Resident visited the site recently and can confirm that the monument has fallen into a serious state of decay and disrepair.

Graffiti has gradually spread around the walls of the building with messages painted in red suggesting that visitors should keep away. Words such as private, family and dog can be read in English.

We tried to speak to the family by knocking on a side door to the convent, but no one answered. Access to the inside of the convent was virtually impossible with doors and windows bricked up and dense vegetation blocking entry."[1]

A petition was set up, but to date nothing seems to have happened to the old convent, which still lies abandoned overlooking the town below. I often wonder what happened to the old man and his family that we met there that day, and we felt quite honoured that he chose to let us enter the site and look around.

---

1. Portugal Resident (02.01.2012). Website article by Inês Lopes *Petition to Save Abandoned National Monument*. Accessed 1st March 2020 through https://www.portugalresident.com/petition-to-save-abandoned-national-monument/

33

Festivals and Fairs

There are so many local fairs and festivals here you really are spoilt for choice. Whether you want to celebrate chocolate, sardines, flowers, sweet potatoes or farming, there will be an event somewhere for you during the calendar year.

Our favourite event of the year happens every August when the town of Silves is transported back to medieval times for ten days, with feasting, dancing, jousting and shopping.

Arriving at Silves it is not long before you are caught up in the excitement of it all. If you park in the municipal car park near the swimming pool you can help the fund-raising of the local Bombeiros by paying 2 euros and then walk past the river to one of the fair's ticket booths. The event is ticket only but for 2 euros for an evening's entry to the town, or only 4 euros for a wrist band for the entire 10 days, this is extremely good value.

Shows cost extra; the jousting tournament and entry ticket is 5 euros, or you can pay 5 euros for entry plus castle entertainment which is usually a professional circus theatre group. You could even go the whole way and pay 60 euros (adult) or 30 euros (child age 6-10) for a 'Medieval Experience' which includes a costume, entry to all the events and shows with an escort, a medieval banquet and a souvenir. You can even rent a costume for the night for only 3 euros (adult) or 2 euros (child) which is very good value as the costumes are quite impressive!

It is hard to know where to begin once you arrive there are so many things to see and experience. If you do not have a show to catch which have set times, then you are free to wander around. The area around the Praça Al-Muthamid gardens is transformed into a tented area and includes games and events for families and children to enjoy, including traditional archery (watch out for stray flying arrows!).

Each night re-enacts a different part of the history of this town, which was the ancient capital of the Algarve. The show covers the period from 1189 during the reign of Sancho I, with the first Christian conquest of the city through to 1191 with the Muslim re-conquest.

The re-enactments are wonderfully acted by a professional drama company. At 6 p.m. each evening the events commence with a procession through the streets which starts from the Praça Al-Muthamid gardens and winds its way all the way to the top of the town outside the cathedral.

At 6.30 p.m. there is a small drama enacted in front of the cathedral and then it is a feast of colour, drama, events and stories all evening. It's fair to say that it can be quite hard to know what is happening where; many times you can turn a corner to find a dance troupe or drumming group have just finished a set, although we have found that if you ask a group they usually know where they are going to be and at what time - so just ask!

There are so many different groups performing around the event including a medieval dance group, and a circus theatre group who are the main event in the castle each evening. There are belly dancers, a medieval music group, a drumming group, troubadours, and Egyptian dancers, not to mention the travelling actors who wander the streets re-enacting slavery, drunkenness and general medieval life!

The streets are transformed into a series of market stalls, bazaars and food stalls, selling all manner of crafts, homemade goods and wonderful items. You can even exchange your euros for Xelbs which were the local currency at the time, and with a pleasing exchange rate of 1:1, it is a shopper's paradise!

Food is plentiful and good value. Be prepared to 'buy' your flagon or pottery cup for your drink and to leave a hefty deposit on the pottery roof tile 'plates' that your food is served on - the deposit is refundable upon return. We paid 7 euros for a plate of *mista do carne* (a mixed meat platter) and 7 euros for two meat kebabs, and drinks are usually only 1 euro for a refill of your cup. You then hunker down on a straw bale beside everyone else and tuck in – it is great fun!

The Jousting Tournament is ticket only and good value for an hour's entertainment. I would say it is particularly well suited for families and has a good balance of humour and storytelling with some mean feats of horse-riding and dexterity.

One word of advice - wear something sensible on your feet! The cobbles are notoriously slippery in Silves and there is a lot of climbing up and sliding down steep streets to negotiate if you want to get the full flavour of this event.

The event runs from 6 p.m. each evening, until 1 a.m. On Fridays and Saturdays they are open until 2 p.m. and on the final night there is a closing show at midnight in front of the cathedral, complete with fireworks.

We can heartily recommend this event as an experience not to be missed. For us it is the highlight of the summer events held across the Algarve, and some years we go every night!

❀ ❧ ❀ ❦ ❀

Another event that we never miss is Loulé Carnaval, which is reported to be the oldest carnival in Portugal. It is like having a small slice of Brazilian carnival on the doorstep. Many towns and villages celebrate carnival, but Loulé is far and away the biggest and best for the Algarve.

The shops are awash with carnival outfits and wigs from early February and the Portuguese seem to adore their Carnaval weekend.

The first time we went to Loulé Carnaval we went armed with cameras, some friends and some silly hats, alongside the most amazing sunshine and hot weather on a bright and clear Saturday in February. We arrived early at Loulé (and you need to arrive early as parking is almost impossible later.)

The Carnaval itself starts at 3 p.m. and there was quite a queue for the tickets to enter the segregated roads, but 2 euros for an adult ticket seemed great value.

The crowds soon gathered, and it became very busy by the time everything started. The floats are all enormous and very professional with hours and hours of work going into each one. They are pulled by tractors along the main street in a big circuit. It takes over an hour for them all to pass you by and they go around three times!

The theme of the Carnaval changes each year, usually they have a very political theme. There is a free brochure that comes with your tickets and it is well worth picking up as it explains the theme of each float in Portuguese and English. It is very useful to pick up the smaller nuances and themes that are the theme of each float. Political messages and statements abound.

One year the then leaders of the ruling coalition, Pedro Passos Coelho and Paulo Portas, sat together on top of a large military tank, whilst the Defence Minister, Aguiar Branco, attempted to protect the nation with a single slingshot – which was a direct reference to the recent Defence spending cuts in Portugal.

Not all the floats are political though, the Garden of Eden passed us by one year although I did find Eve a rather scary looking creature! Perhaps that had something to do with the giant toadstool in her garden?!

It feels very safe but be aware that the floats pass by very close to you in the crowd. With all the streamers, music, dancing, and carnival atmosphere it is great fun and very noisy! Watch out for a shower of streamers, coins or sweets onto the heads of the crowd from some of the floats.

The lovely thing about the Carnaval is that most of the children, and quite a few adults in the crowd dress up and really enjoy themselves. You can often see children scampering around collecting all the streamers and glitter - and sweets - that land on the ground.

Every float and dance troupe have children and adults in fantastic costumes singing and dancing. Some of the 'costumes' are a little 'brief' to put it politely, and I am sure there is a lot of body paint used up each day!

The mixture of political satire, music, dancing and party streamers seems to sum up the mood of the carnival atmosphere. Even though the average Portuguese worker's wage is low, and people often work long hours, yet still the people come out and party, and often there's even time for a quick conga along the route. It really is a spectacle of colour, music, dance and life, and an event we try to visit each year.

✿ﻬ✿✧✿

At the other end of the calendar year, the 11th of November in Portugal is *Dia da São Martinho*, (St Martin's day), which is celebrated with roast chestnuts. Traditionally it is also the day marked in the calendar for the opening and tasting of the new year's wine.

St Martin has two great legends attached to him and the first is his apparent reluctance to become a bishop! The story goes that he hid in a barn hoping to escape the people coming to make him a bishop, but a flock of geese made such a noise that they gave up his hiding place … I have fun imagining the modern-day version of this with the Archbishop of Canterbury hiding away … and so the goose became St Martin's animal symbol.

He is also famous for cutting his cloak in half in a snowstorm to stop a beggar from freezing to death. The next night, he had a dream in which he saw Jesus wearing the half of the cloak he'd given away, surrounded by angels. The remaining piece of cloak became a very revered relic, and the building where his cloak or 'cappa' in Latin, was preserved, was known as the 'cappella', which is the root of our words chapel and chaplain. St Martin therefore became the patron saint of beggars.

It's also both the start of winter and a time to celebrate harvest time, hence the traditional tasting of the new wine on this day.

According to history the 11th November was also the last day before a fast period lasting 40 days, called in Latin the 'Quadragesima Sancti Martini', or the 'forty days of St. Martin'. On St. Martin's day people ate and drank heartily for a last time before they started to fast. This period of fasting was later shortened and called 'Advent' by the Church.

Today it is seen as a mini-carnival day, called *Magusto* with feasting, lanterns and bonfires across most of Europe. In Portugal they also drink an alcoholic beverage called *água-pé* (which literally translates as 'foot water'), made by adding water to the remains left after the juice is pressed out of the grapes for wine – which is traditionally done by stomping on them in vats with bare feet, and letting it ferment for several days.

There's another St Martin's day tradition, the belief that the day heralds a period of warm weather called *'Verão de São Martinho'* ('St. Martin's Summer') and that it will be nice and sunny all the way to Christmas. Now that sounds like a good tradition to celebrate!

One of the biggest local fairs happens almost opposite our village. The St Martin's Fair takes place at the Parque de Feiras e Exposições in Portimão and runs for ten days. This fair has been celebrated in Portimão since 1662 which is an incredible tradition.

As you enter the fairground you are greeted with the sight of lots of stalls selling steaming hot chestnuts. You can buy a dozen for 2 euros in a paper bag. There's quite an art to steaming them over the hot coals and the smell and the smoke are quite enticing.

Tradition holds that the festival is also a time of ancient sacrifice to honour the dead and a time to prepare, at midnight, a table with chestnuts for deceased family members to eat. I'm not sure we could wait that long; they don't tend to last very long in the packet once we have bought them!

The main area is devoted to the fairground with a big wheel dominating the skyline. The one thing that never fails to fascinate us about these types of events is that virtually every stall sells the same thing ... there are rows of food stalls and they all sell ...my favourite *faturas* and *churros* (a fried-dough pastry).

It's not a huge complaint though as they are delicious! You can also buy waffles and candy floss, and there are some catering stands at the rear of the fair selling hot food with seating areas.

It is a child's delight here, there are so many stalls and stands and fairground rides for all ages! Rides usually cost 2 euros each, except for two days which have special priced tickets for children and families respectively. Entrance is free however which is a nice touch.

Some of the rides are quite spectacular and make for some great photographs especially once it gets dark - including some rides which would not be for the faint-hearted!

It's a very noisy, busy, event, there is music playing at full volume from all angles - not to mention the screams of excitement (and fear?!) from the rides!

It's not all rides though, there are a range of market stalls and things to buy and browse through - from traditional arts and crafts, to 'knock-off' sunglasses – 'Kay-Ban' sunglasses anyone?!

And a ridiculously large number of stalls again all selling the same thing ... like shoes and clothing ... toys and gimmicks ... and the biggest wooden spoons we have ever seen!

Walking past a van with its washing hung outside brings home the reality that for many people that have stalls at fairs like this, they lead a transient and difficult lifestyle that is hardly very romantic and involves a lot of setting up, running, unpacking and moving along to the next fair.

It sits rather strangely alongside the main indoor arena of the venue which hosts an exhibition of new and used cars. To be honest we have no idea why they are there, it doesn't seem to 'fit' at all, although we suppose it gives the adults something different to look at while the children are busy on the funfair.

There is just time for another bag of chestnuts before we leave and a last look around the fairground with its bright lights, and bustling atmosphere until next year. And the promise that Christmas is just around the corner.

34

Christmas in the Algarve

Christmas here in the Algarve is a gentle affair, which is fine by me, as I do not like the commercial hype that surrounds the festive season that seems to begin in early September in the UK. Here you are relatively safe until the beginning of November, although the major supermarkets and store promotions seem to be getting earlier each year.

There are many enjoyable and gentle Christmas Fairs that pop up, many selling original crafts and gifts. You can celebrate 'Bavarian style' with a local German beer festival, alongside lovely little street markets complete with stalls selling local produce and crafts, roasted chestnuts and sweet pastries, mulled wine, and all accompanied with musical entertainment. Christmas seems less 'corporate' in Portugal, and far more about creative initiatives and local people coming together.

Another tradition you will see everywhere is Santa Claus or *Pai Natal* who is usually to be found scampering up the side of a building or patio as a toy on a ladder. It must be confusing to be a small child in Portugal though as tradition says that the presents are brought by the new-born Jesus, so I am not sure what role Santa plays out here – he always looks like a burglar to me!

Christmas is a showcase of lighting here, and you will find sparkling lights and displays hanging in most major towns. One year we were delighted to walk around Lagoa one evening, quite by chance, and gasped in wonder at their Christmas town display. They had giant metal angels covered in twinkling lights lining the streets. They were spectacular. We discovered later that Lisbon has a new display of lights and features every year, and the following year some lucky towns are given the displays. Lagoa hit the jackpot that year with its angel display.

Ferragudo sadly never quite matches up to that display, however one year had me stifling my giggles at their main display, which was set for all to admire at the entrance to the square. A grass area had been transformed with three giant polystyrene figures that were lit inside with a myriad of small twinkling lights. So far, no problem.

The first figure, standing about 20-foot-high, was of a little drummer boy, complete with red costume and drum. A suitable theme. Sadly the other two figures didn't quite fit the Christmas brief - the first was a giant elephant - and the second - a panda. Well, they are not exactly native to Portugal, and I am sure I would have remembered if the traditional nativity scene had a panda and elephant stood alongside the camels and sheep. Oh dear. I'm not sure where they came from, but I do hope the Câmara didn't spend too much of their money on them. We were still giggling about them with a local Portuguese friend well into March the following year.

✧ɷ✧ જ✧

The Living Statues or '*Estátuas Vivas no Natal*' herald in the start of Christmas for us, as they visit Lagoa early in December for two days. Their display around the local streets is remarkable, their costumes are exquisite, and these street artists stand - perfectly still in most cases - for three hours (with only small breaks halfway through). From Mozart, to chimney sweeps riding magical bikes, to chestnut sellers, lovers, and fairies hidden in the trees, this is one event not to be missed.

Each year their costumes and themes, which change every year, are incredible; and it is lovely to watch the faces of young children light up as they pass by a statue that suddenly reaches out to them and hands them a batten to conduct the orchestra, or hands them a shiny orange from a basket of fruit. Kat the dog absolutely loves this event and will spend ages sat in front of a statue waiting for them to move!

❄〰❄〰❄

On Christmas Eve, a family dinner known as the *consoada* is celebrated with great enthusiasm. The word represents the meal that is taken at the end of a day's fasting and derives from the Latin word 'consolare', meaning 'to comfort'. Traditionally Advent is also referred to as 'little Lent', because, like Lent, it is a time of repentance and fasting. The four-week fast leading up to Christmas however has mostly been replaced by this one special Christmas Eve meal for most families.

In some areas it is the custom for people to reserve places at the table set for the 'Consoada' supper for those relatives who have recently passed away. Some families light a *cepo de Natal* (Christmas log), which is a large piece of oak that burns on the hearth.

Traditionally, the Christmas Eve supper consists of abstaining from meat dishes. The traditional fish is *bacalhau* (salted cod), but other regions eat *polvo* (octopus), or another fish dish. The highlight of the meal, with all the family sat around the table, must be the many desserts that follow the main meal. The *Bolo Rei* (King cake), is unique with its round shape, with a hole in the centre, shaped like a crown. Inside is a kind of sweet brioche-like bread made with eggs, and filled with nuts, dried fruits, and raisins and topped with candied fruit and powdered sugar.

It represents the gifts that the Magi gave to baby Jesus when he was born: the crust symbolises the gold, the candied and dried fruit symbolises the myrrh and the aroma of the cake is there to represent the incense. It is traditionally eaten between 24th December and January 6 (Epiphany). Traditionally, there is also a dried fava bean inside the cake; luckily this is usually a large bean. The family tradition says that whoever has the slice with the fava bean is the King and must buy or bake next year's cake. Hopefully they also don't have to pay out for any dental treatments resulting from crunching down on the hard bean!

✿🐚✿🐚✿

There is something magical about the traditional *presépio* (nativity crib) here in Portugal and you will find them displayed everywhere from the front window of the smallest house or shop window, through to giant and life-sized displays that abound in the towns and cities ... including the extraordinary *presépio* at Vila Real de Santo António which has over 5,500 figures.

We visited the tiny village of Alferce, near Monchique one year and found the most exquisite and intricately detailed – and huge – *presépio* in the main square in the village.

The first nativity crib was created by Saint Francis in Greccio, Italy in 1223 and featured real people and animals, and Alferce obviously used this as the idea behind their own elaborate display.

We were greeted by the three Magi on their camels entering the village and we suddenly realised that although this is a tiny village, they take their nativity very seriously.

Next came a shepherd and his sheep and then the farmer and his donkey, and more sheep. All the figures and animals were life-size and very realistic. Hours of work had obviously gone into painstakingly creating all these figures with elaborate costumes and details.

But then we entered the square and we were greeted with the most amazing sight: an enormous miniature village scene recreated with the most amazing attention to detail, with houses, figures, animals and rural life in its entirety. The water feature even had live fish!

Many of the figures were mechanical and really brought everything to life. We kept looking more closely at each figure to see what they were portraying, there were so many tiny little cameos of rural life brought magically to life. Local features and trades were also included, with a baker and potter, people plying their trade and even a game of cards being played most energetically by four men sat at a table.

When you looked closely at some of the figures you could see the brilliant details adorning these tiny figurines which were mostly made of carved wood and painted so beautifully.

The three Kings heralded the advent of Christ's birth, carrying their gifts of course; and the main event, the cradle with Mary and Joseph, were beautifully portrayed with a glowing backlight. Tradition states that the baby Jesus is not added to the crib until Christmas morning.

We were also interested to see lots of *searinhas*, or small wheat sprigs, which were displayed around the crib. We have discovered this is a tradition in the Algarve; it symbolises asking the baby Jesus to bless your home and to provide for all your household's needs for the year ahead.

This was a stunning display for such a small village, and the local people were rightly proud of their fantastic nativity. Visiting it was a lovely way to remember what Christmas means to many people here.

❄❅❄❆❄

Christmas Day itself is often a quiet family affair in Portugal, and many people take to the beach in the afternoon for a stroll, often in brilliant sunshine. We have often just worn a T-shirt and jeans and enjoyed the beautiful blue skies and warmth of the sun as we walk along, smiling and wishing everyone we pass '*Feliz Natal*' (Merry Christmas).

For several years our tradition has been to go to the Christmas Day Santa Swim at Armação de Pêra. Our favourite Holiday Inn hotel organises this charity event and it is quite a sight to see around 200 people wearing Santa costumes all lined up ready to run into the sea for a swim! Many people launch right into the cold waves, although there are lots of people that just paddle in the surf. There is a real party atmosphere to the event which usually has at least another 200 people just watching from the side-lines. It certainly is one way of celebrating the festive occasion.

And then suddenly it is over. There is no Boxing Day here in Portugal, the 26th December is a normal working day, which suits us fine. No stringing it all out and sitting around bored at home.

New Year's Eve is celebrated with parties and fireworks and blue (or red) underwear! Tradition dictates that you select underwear of a specific colour to wear at midnight whilst eating 12 raisins (and making 12 wishes!) as the clock counts down its last 12 strokes of the year. Blue underwear will bring you good luck and a little red number will ensure you have love in the year ahead.

You had better swallow the raisins quickly as the fireworks that are set off to herald the New Year are going to be a loud and brash affair. There is no hiding from this moment, across the Algarve towns and villages herald the new year with a dazzling and loud display. One of the biggest events always occurs at Albufeira on the beach, where live music and a spectacular firework display ensures that thousands of people flock to the area to celebrate. The events are always free as well and everyone seems to enjoy themselves.

For those with pets however, it can be a terrible night. Poor Kat the dog is like most animals, and she does not like the loud bangs and noise. If I am there to comfort her, she is not too bad, and soon settles down to sleep again once the noise has faded into the night. We certainly would not leave her alone at night on New Year's Eve.

Dave is happy to jump around on the balcony outside shooting the dazzling displays that light up the sky all around us. From our balcony we get a bird's eye view of the main Portimão display as it is set off from the conference centre roof just below us. Add to that the displays of Ferragudo, Praia da Rocha, Carvoeiro, Albufeira and even Vilamoura, which can all be seen from our little balcony. There certainly is no escape for poor Kat.

I am always startled by another loud local tradition that happens each New Year's Eve. At midnight lots of our neighbours clamber up to their balconies carrying pots and pans and spoons and proceed to bang them as loudly as they can to ward away evil spirits. They usually wait until the fireworks have finished, and the first year we were stood on our balcony and it happened, it frightened the life out of me!

Just remember when you go back home to enter the front door with your right foot first for good luck of course.

New Year's Day gives the chance to exercise another tradition, for if you are feeling brave, and not too hungover, then another dip in the cold Atlantic Ocean is the order of the day. The Holiday Inn hotel also host an annual charity New Year's Day swim. Pyjamas are an optional costume for this event, although it is always amusing to see people of all ages and sized running into the water, some wearing onesies and clutching their favourite teddy bear, and squealing as the cold water hits them full on.

These charity swims are well supported events and raise lots of money for local worthwhile causes. Dave has happily been the official photographer there for many years at both the Christmas and New year events; although I have to say I have never actually been brave (or should that read - daft) enough to actually go for a swim ... I know how cold that water can be!

35

Permanent Residents

"**C**an it really be five years ago that we gained our 5-year residency paperwork?"

Well that was the question I asked Dave as we realised that our temporary residency which lasts for five years was about to expire and we could now apply for our Permanent Residence Certificate or *'Certificado de Residência Permanente'* from the Foreigners and Borders Service or SEF *'Serviço de Estrangeiros e Fronteiras'* office. The certificate lasts for ten years and is renewable.

Well we knew that much information and gaining our five-year residency had been a pretty painless experience so off we went to start the process ... and this chapter is the result of all our research, teeth-grinding, hang-wringing and long periods of waiting. Be warned ... it's a long story and that seems about right for the process we went through ... one that, in theory, should have been quite simple to execute.

But the good news was that at the end of all the bureaucratic pain ... we would then officially 'legal' for the next ten years. So if you are in a similar position our advice is ... don't give up hope!!

The biggest hurdle to overcome is getting an appointment at the

SEF office. Our local office is Portimão, and the only other office for the Algarve is based at Faro, so it depends where you live as to which office you are under - and don't try to book in at the wrong one. The official position for booking an appointment is that you can either log on to the SEF website or you can call them on their outrageous 'price per minute' helpline available from 9 a.m. – 5.30 p.m. (Monday-Friday)

Well after about a week of trying to book online we gave up as their website just kept coming up with 'Number Error' as a message. Calling the helpline was even worse ... if you managed to get through all you could get was a recorded message spoken in Portuguese at a super-fast speed ... Press 1 for residency ... Press 3 for the Algarve ... Press 7 if you have lost the will to live yet ... Press 9 ... oh sorry no we are going to move over to an engaged tone now and annoy the heck out of you ... please call back later.

In desperation I said to Dave,

"Hang on a minute, we only live 5 minutes' drive from the SEF office ... we'll just go in there and book an appointment."

Oh how naive of me! We went there, took a ticket (obligatory of course) and sat waiting for about half an hour, with a rather bemused expression on our faces ... what are all the different options for on the TV screen?! ... you can have any letter from A to J ... all different ... all relating back to the people clutching tickets sat on the plastic chairs that might have been there since the previous week. One woman had a picnic lunch with her – oh dear, that really should have been a warning sign for us.

We eventually got to the desk relating to our now crumpled ticket ... to be met with a miserable lady we immediately named 'Mrs Happy'. She informed us that the only way we could get an appointment ... at the actual SEF office ... that we were currently sat in ... at the very desk no.7 that we were currently sat at ... with the very woman we were sat in front of ... was to ... wait for it ... call the national helpline number or use the SEF website.

We explained that we had been trying to do that for the last two weeks ... that our 5-year residency was about to run out in three weeks' time … and that could we just book an appointment with her there? Oh no! She 'helpfully' gave us an email we could use instead to book an appointment through …. and that was it. Meeting over.

Needless to say … we tried the email she gave us … and after about five days … we got a reply …. telling us … yes, you've guessed it … we could call the national helpline number or use the SEF website.

Desperation set in! We searched online and found out that we were not alone, and that lots of people were struggling to get an appointment. Then, rather randomly, someone on Facebook said that they just went in to the Portimão SEF and asked them what to do … and got an appointment booked in directly with the lady at the desk! There was much gnashing of teeth when we read that one! Then a friend airily told us,

"Oh, I just took all the paperwork in ready, I didn't have an appointment, they just did it there and then for me …"

And research online also suggested that going via an indirect route to the SEF office at Faro might be an option for some reason … well – not the actual office of course. The appointments for SEF in Faro can also be made by going to something called the CNAI group office adjacent to the SEF offices in the Faro Municipal Market. We cannot tell you definitively whether this would work or not as we didn't want to drive all the way to Faro to be told that they could only do bookings for the Faro area and not Portimão.

So I sat one afternoon working on the computer randomly pressing my F5 refresh button on the SEF booking page and then suddenly … I had put Dave's details in … (I kept swopping between us!) and it went through, and there it was … a message came up telling me to 'pick a date and time for your appointment'. Blimey! I quickly pressed the first option available and registered his email … two minutes later we had received an email confirming Dave's appointment!!!

'Great!' I thought and went back to book one for me … yes, you've guessed it – no chance!!! After about two more days of trying, I gave up and having asked friends who had been through the same process in Beja a few weeks before ... and who confirmed that they both went in under one booking as they are married and have shared finances ... we thought 'go for it!'. We risked it and left it at the one appointment ... it was like rocking horse poop and we guarded the date and time jealously in the diary.

The appointment was dated about ten days after our 5-year residency had expired but 'Mrs Happy' had assured us that it would not be a problem if we were late as she slid over the useless email address to us. There wasn't much we could do about it anyway so we didn't worry too much ... apart from friends teasing us that we would be 'illegal aliens' and have to start the 5-year process again (!!!!) ... (Postscript – we were fine!)

We then had about three weeks to gather everything together that we needed. 'Mrs Happy' had given us a tiny scrap of paper with a list of items of paperwork that we would apparently require ... it wasn't much use I have to say. She also gave us tatty photocopies of the obligatory forms which had to be completed in advance. Luckily some friends saved the day and sent us over the information they had been given when they applied for their residency, which turned out to be spot on.

✿෨✿രଠ

You can select the form you have to complete online on the SEF site and then print it out and fill it in. Most of it has an English translation incorporated, and the non-translated section on one of the pages we left blank and it was completed for us when we got there; as it is about the legislation around residency and we were unsure which boxes to tick.

And the list of documents you need to take with the form? Well it was a long list of course!

Two passport sized colour photos. It is quite hard to find somewhere that still does passport photos the old-fashioned way in this new digital photographic era, but we did manage it. You need a white background ... and no-one seemed to know whether you can smile in or not in your photograph, so I went for an enigmatic Mona Lisa look (!) and Dave grinned happily. He was far more interested in what camera they had, and which programme the shop were using to process the images. The photographer is never off duty.

You must have a photocopy of your passport and of course we had no idea whether this had to be in colour or would black and white suffice … so we did colour copies to be on the safe side.

We also needed another *'Atestado De Residência'* form completed by our local Junta de Freguesia or parish council. From previous experience we thought this would be more complicated than it was, and we had no idea what we needed to take with us for permanent residency, so we took everything we could think of. It turned out to be a straightforward form they complete for you which you collect a few days later once it has been signed and sealed.

The Atestado application form is filled in at the Junta while you are there and they even ask you for the full names of your parents, which seems a pretty strange thing to ask a grown man of 61 to complete! Everything gets photocopied and stapled to death and the form itself only costs 4 euros each – a bargain.

We also had to prove our means of subsistence; we still do not know how much money you actually have to have shown in order to tick a magic imaginary box somewhere, but we asked our accountant for help with this one and she sent us back our latest filed and completed tax returns. We are both sole traders and file an annual return so that made things quite simple … apart from the 16 pages of A4 we each had to print out … and we also took copies of Dave's P60s for the periods covering the same financial year as well.

Our friends made us smile, as they told us that when they went to fill in their paperwork the husband had to complete a form to agree to be financially responsible for his wife as she has no income here of her own except his pension. She was not impressed!!

We had to have our Fiscal and Social Security numbers and as we are taxpayers the social security number information was already on our tax returns … but we photocopied it separately from the Social Security paperwork too (we were taking no chances here!)

We also had to take our current five-year residency paperwork with us, and we had photocopied it ready for the meeting, but they take your original copy and keep it, so it was a good job we had taken our original versions with us. Of course they don't tell you that until you get there for your appointment, I almost kept our originals at home as a souvenir of our first five years here; so it was a good job I'm not that sentimental!

The 10-year residency costs only 15 euros, and we took cash with us as so many official government offices don't seem to have cash card machines. We put it with all the paperwork required and the form we had completed for each of us. All stashed into a small wheelbarrow which we pushed into the SEF office on the allotted date and time.

We were still nervous about two of us sneaking in under one booking on the day ... well we were lucky, and we think we now know why some people had been luckier than us up to this point once we arrived there. We had an appointment for 10 a.m. so we thought that we would get there a little early ... stories of our friends waiting four hours to be seen were ringing in our ears that morning as we contemplated taking a book to read ... or some food ... to keep us going.

Well we took the obligatory ticket at 9.49 a.m. (Tip: the smiling Security Man is very helpful!) ... we were number E001 ... we looked up on the screen and saw that desk 7 was registered at number E013 ... and we thought 'uh-oh, we're in for a long wait'. Then suddenly the counter tipped round and reverted to 001 ... and we were up! Straight in and up to the desk where we sat down expectantly. We were a little stunned to be honest as we had expected to be there for ages waiting and the lady at the desk was a different lady ... not 'Mrs Happy' ... this lady was genuinely nice and helpful. She went through all our paperwork requirements, ticked everything off, we paid our 15 euros each ... and at 10:06 a.m. we were walking back out of the door clutching a receipt each ... having been told that they would call us when the forms were ready to be collected and that it would be 'about 2 weeks'. (The legal requirement is that it should be ready for collection within 15 days).

And that was that!

Well, sort of … tick forward two weeks and we got the call to collect our forms with the exhortation that there was,

"No need to book, just come in."

Well that sounded ominous and sure enough when we got there, we were given ticket numbers B0041 and B0042 … and good old desk 7 was only on B0028. We went for a coffee at a nearby café and came back 15 minutes later and the display had inched on to number B0029. We drew lots and I won, Dave stayed in the queue and I scampered over to the Pingo Doce supermarket on the other side of the road to do the weekly food shopping. We figured we had plenty of time to wait!!

I was happily at the checkout paying when suddenly Dave called me and said,

"You'd better come back quick … we are up!"

I paid, scampered back to the car with the trolley, loaded the car, abandoned the trolley, ran back over there to find Dave sat at desk 7 … with yes you've guessed it, 'Mrs Happy' who was being as miserable as ever and threatening to make me take another ticket and wait again! I sat quickly down into the seat, tried to look pitiful, and she reneged and did my form for me, which involved lots of signatures and a wonky fingerprint.

And that's it! Suddenly you are legal for the next ten years … and you have a silly piece of tri-folded card that you are miraculously supposed to keep in a pristine condition … for ten years!!! I doubted that mine would last ten months! We went back to our lovely local Junta and got them to do a certified copy of them for us the same as they do for a passport … that way we thought we might be able to keep the original looking half-decent for a while.

Our ten-year permanent residency. And despite all the administrative pain … it was worth it, as it is a great feeling knowing that we can live here officially for the next ten years.

Next up in our list of things to do was to start finding out about gaining dual citizenship before the dreaded Brexit happened … which you can now apply for after only five years of consecutive residency. Let's hope we don't have to go back to the same desk at the SEF for that one!

(Postscript: since our adventures with SEF, they have now updated the system and you now receive a credit-card sized residency card with all your information included in one place. Sadly they have not replaced the online booking system or 'Mrs Happy.')

36

Selling and Buying Again

O ur house had served us well, but for many reasons it felt the right time to think about selling and buying something a little smaller. Our hearts and lives were firmly set on remaining in Portugal, long before the Brexit vote happened. The outcome, and subsequent shambles however, certainly helped to cement our position, and gave us the impetus to secure our permanent future home here in the sunshine.

One of the things that has always astounded me is the commission fees charged by estate agents in Portugal. I have had numerous conversations with agents who have tried, and failed, to convince me that their work is so different to the equivalent in the UK and try to justify their 5% + IVA rates. When I tell them that agents in the UK often charge around 1% or sometimes even lower, (with no added tax) their faces usually change colour; their chests almost always puff out slightly and they often become very defensive.

Which should leave you unsurprised to find out that we were determined to try to sell our house ourselves, with no estate agent in the middle. There is no legal reason for an agent, although it is less common to find people selling privately here. Undaunted I set about the challenge with relish, and the maths certainly helped with this decision, as 5% + IVA in commission fees is a lot of money!

Having a professional photographer for a husband, who shoots real estate, also helped, and we soon had a snazzy online brochure set up, and a shiny big banner on the front garden wall. We also knew that Facebook could be our friend, and realising that there were no groups set up specifically for private property sales here, we set up an Algarve Property for Sale (by owner) Facebook group which had a nice big 'No Agents' banner along the top of the page - just to make sure they were under no illusions! We had lots of agents of course instantly trying to join, some even said they were not an estate agent when they answered the joining questions which we had set up ... but their Facebook profile picture had their estate agency's logo in the background! To date, we have over 2,000 members - and no agents!

Nothing happens quickly here, so we were happy to settle down and wait for a sale. We had several seriously interested parties, although sadly none were able to buy straight away; but we became quite adept at showing people round and answering questions. We always knew that we had a lovely home, it was a good solid property with fantastic views in a sought-after location, and it would just take the right people to come along and fall in love with it as we had.

After a few months we had a lovely couple contact us who already knew Ferragudo well and wanted to stay in the area. They came, went away, came back, brought a builder round to discuss renovation ideas, came back again, and then suddenly we had accepted an offer and we were up and running.

We had decided right at the start of the process that we would not even start to look at the market until we had accepted an offer and had a serious buyer. Although I occasionally had a sneaky look at the market online; it seemed pointless going to view a property, maybe really liking it, and then not being able to be able to buy it. I'm a firm believer in timing, and things happening for a reason ... which was a good thing to hold on to, especially as events unfolded for us.

Our buyers made us an offer in the April, and we set a date a couple of weeks later to complete the 10% deposit and promissory contract. The system here I think is a good one, as a buyer you put down a 10% deposit and contracts are signed. If the buyer reneges, they lose their deposit, however if a seller changes their mind and withdraws, they must pay back 20% to the buyers. It's a serious moment and a serious amount of money. Usually the full sale then goes through quite quickly, however our buyers were also selling their own property, and had already agreed with their buyers that they would have a completion date of Friday 13th September (yes I know!) and would we be ok with waiting until that date for completion? It gave us four months to find somewhere else to buy, which suited us very well and we were happy to agree to this. With hindsight it is a good job we had that long …

We initially started by writing out a list of requirements for our next property. We were very clear on what we didn't want … which was a good starting point. We had also whittled it down to a shortlist of three areas we wanted to concentrate our search within, which is one of the real benefits of already knowing the Algarve region well. We certainly knew where we didn't want to live! We viewed several properties across a range of different conditions and locations, found one possible property which we put an offer in for, only for the agent to tell us that our offer, only 7,500 euros below the asking price was not enough. Alarm bells rang and we walked away.

✿ᔍ✿ଓ✿

And then we found what we thought would be the perfect smaller property, on the edge of a small hamlet, not far from Silves, which was one of our chosen areas. We viewed it with the agent, and it all seemed great, the rooms were just about big enough, but outside it had a large garden with space ready for an art studio to be built at the end of the plot, and it even had a small swimming pool. And all well within our budget.

It seemed too good to be true, it had been recently remodelled, and it was ready to move into. We put in an offer which was accepted, we chatted to a friend who happened to live nearby and who confirmed that location was a good one, and then we instructed our solicitor to start the paperwork.

We also, unusually for buyers out here, brought in one of only two surveyors that work in the Algarve (that tells you how popular surveys are!) and asked him to do his worst. Looking back this was the best 500 euros we had ever spent. Just as the solicitor was about to draw up the Promissory Contract, the survey came back, in great detail, with concerns over the structure of the lounge area which turned out to be an extension.

Our solicitor, almost in passing, then said to us,

"There isn't a pool, is there?"

"Erm, yes there is," we replied.

"Well, it's not on the plans." came her reply.

Several hurried phone calls later and an indeterminable wait ensued while things were checked out. No, there had been no authorisation for a swimming pool, it was shown as a septic tank on the plans. And the extension? Well, we never did find out whether it was legal or not. It had certainly been added later than the original building.

Silves Câmara is notorious for its attitude to pools, extensions, and added structures (bang went my plans for an art studio in the garden) and if they had investigated and found the swimming pool; as the new owners we would have been held responsible for paying the fines all the way back to the day the Câmara decided the pool (and also the extension) had been added. It was, indeed, too good to be true, and we walked away, luckily none the poorer, but certainly wiser.

That left us in the middle of July, with no house to purchase by September. Plan B was to rent, so we were not unduly concerned, and then Dave said,

"I've found a place in Aljezur, which might be worth a look."

Aljezur was one of our top choices for location, the beaches are fabulous, it is a more unspoilt, rural and quieter area than the main Algarve region, and only 40 minutes away.

Finding a decent, modern, reasonably priced property in Aljezur we had thought was an impossibility though, as so many properties in the old town are just that – old … and in need of work. And we were definite that we wanted to be surrounded by local Portuguese people, as far away from an expat enclave as possible. A tough find we thought, as we drove, almost reluctantly, to view the property Dave had found randomly online.

And then we arrived, looked around us at the beautiful views and peaceful little hamlet of houses situated on the edge of the new village that we had been directed to, and stepped inside a fabulously proportioned, bright and modern house.

We went for a coffee after looking round it all twice, sat down with our wish-list and ticked off absolutely every single one of our 'must-have' requirements; and none of the 'don't want' list. It was perfect, and within budget, allowing us some money left over to do some glaringly obvious jobs that needed attending to.

We put in an offer, negotiated slightly and two days later, our offer was accepted. No chain, no issues, the survey came back fine, the paperwork was drawn up by our patient solicitor, and the Promissory Contract signed and paid. We were on our way!

❊ ❧ ❖ ❦ ❊

Unlike our move from the UK to Portugal, we were far more organised in our planning to pack and move this time around, and we wrote down exactly what furniture and large items we wanted to take with us, and what we were going to leave behind. I began writing lists and planning the move, and excitedly shopping online for new furniture. Our buyers wanted us to leave any furniture we did not want behind, as they were selling their flat fully furnished, so we were free to start from scratch and buy new things that suited our new house. We were also determined to take 'down-sizing' seriously and assessed almost every item in our current house to decide whether we needed it / wanted it / or could remove it. The local charity shop did extremely well that summer.

The vendors for the house we were buying were an odd mix of an older Portuguese man and his foreign girlfriend, who was deeply into voodoo and did not want to move. She certainly made things awkward for us when we visited the property with our preferred decorator, who wanted to view the property in order to quote us for the ensuing paint job that would be required. As we were not completing until mid-September, we wanted the house rendered and painted as soon as possible after moving in, and certainly before any autumn rain was forecast. She wailed and screamed at us, and the windows shook with the force of the door slamming shut when we arrived, even though we had contacted the agent in advance to ask permission to visit, and we didn't actually need to go inside to get the necessary information required for the decorating quote.

We decided that, despite her unhappiness, we needed to visit again to measure up ready for moving day. Knowing whether things like our office furniture would fit into the planned third bedroom office was important; so we took a deep breath, rang the agent and asked to visit again. We waited until the 10% deposit had been paid, in the hope that might assuage her anger a little, although in turned out that we had worried for nothing, as she was out the day we visited again. We breathed a sigh of relief and got the tape measure out.

The plans were coming together nicely, and we were looking forward to designing a brand-new lounge area for our new home. A new Ikea store had recently opened near Faro, so we didn't have to travel all the way to Lisbon anymore. New desks and office furniture were also on the list, together with a new waterbed for both bedrooms! Our old and much-loved waterbed was twenty years old; and we decided to treat ourselves to new beds. If we had realised how much work that decision was to cause, we might have chosen differently.

37

Moving

A waterbed contains about eighty gallons of water, housed in a thick rubber casing that sits inside a solid wooden frame. Once filled, it doesn't move ... for anyone! The bedroom in our current house was on the first floor, with its own balcony overlooking the street. It was an amusing moment attaching a hose to the outside tap, feeding it upstairs and filling the waterbed when we moved in, as neighbours walked past, pointed up at the hose, laughed and walked away. I have no idea what they thought we were doing as waterbeds are not that common out here.

Emptying it, we assumed, would be a simple affair, even if it did mean we would be amusing the neighbours once again. We would simply attach the hose to the bed, draw the water out, and gravity would ensure the water would shoot out of the end of the hose which was dangling over the balcony, drop into the front garden, and drain away into the road outside. Well, that was the plan ...

All went well for a while as the water spurted and poured down the street. And then it stopped. We tried again, and a trickle came out, then nothing. It was easy to see that the mattress still contained a substantial amount of water. We were stuck. And then, as often happens with us, we got the giggles, which didn't help matters.

"Well, we can't leave it here, half empty, so what are we going to do?" I said chuckling.

We have lovely friends that are very practical but live an hour away in the southern Alentejo region. Chris, the husband, affectionately known as Mr Chris as he is a 'gadget man' would have an idea, we were sure. We rang him, and as luck would have it, they were coming down to the Algarve that afternoon, and he said he would bring his water pump with him. Doesn't everyone have a water pump lying around?

Chris and his wife Jan came and dropped off the pump, promising to return later and collect it. We eagerly attached it and switched it on and watched a slow swirl of water make its way over the balcony wall. And then it stopped. The poor pump was doing its best, but we needed something closer to a fire brigade pump for this beast.

Undeterred, we managed to lift the mattress slightly which set the pump running again. Little by little the water trickled out. And then the pump made a whirring noise, sighed and stopped. It had just about removed enough water for us to make the mattress moveable. Just. It was still extraordinarily heavy, but slowly we could lift it up and out of the wooden bed frame. And then we dragged it unceremoniously out onto the balcony.

Dave attacked it with a penknife at this stage, creating a few savage holes at the end nearest the drainage point on the balcony, and we cheered as the water started gushing out and tumbling down into the garden below. We left it running, confident that it would drain away, and went off for a much-needed cup of tea. Half an hour later we returned and began a hilarious dance of jumping on one end and dragging the remaining water out. More giggles ensued as I casually remarked,

"I wonder what the neighbours will think we are doing if they spot us up here dancing around?"

They would have been even more amused if they had walked past about an hour later. The mattress refused to release any more water, as it had a type of sponge matting inside it, which when full, stopped the water in the bed from sloshing around if you turned over in bed.

But now it was just being a nuisance retaining a large amount of water like a stubborn sponge.

There was only one thing for it; we would have to heave and pull the mattress up and over the terrace wall and let it crash to the ground below. Then we could drag it down to the bins at the corner of the road. We got it about halfway up and over the wall by sheer determination and effort. It was the heaviest thing I have ever tried to lift. Halfway up and we got the giggles again. Oh dear, this was really going to be a long afternoon. Finally gravity took over, we had it past the pivotal point, we aimed it as best we could onto the path area below, and then we let it drop with a huge crash.

We scampered downstairs, opened the front door, and there it was, a giant shiny blue polybag on the ground - lying in the perfect shape of a curled-up body.

"The neighbours are going to think we have killed someone," I giggled, "it looks exactly like a dead body wrapped up."

It was so funny that we took photos of it before we dragged it all the way up the road and left it by the bins. Rubbish collection out here is thankfully a very forgiving occupation and all sorts of things are left at the bins for 'recycling' or removal. We just hoped that they were in a good mood when they made their rounds that evening; and didn't look too closely at the body bag left beside the bins.

✿ⰰ✿ⰰ✿

We planned our packing and moving days carefully. We had the removal company booked for the Thursday, with completion day for the sale of our house set for the Friday. The packing up was made more complicated by the fact we were leaving lots of items of furniture behind. Several weeks of packing slowly had of course descended into madness three days before the end, when last-minute items were hurriedly packed into the last boxes. We seemed to have a lot of boxes, which were all carefully marked with the destination room and contents inside.

Major pieces of furniture and other items that were not going with us were marked with a big 'X' which translated for the removal company as 'do not load' ... and one entire room had been designated the 'do not pack' room. It was as organised as it could be.

The removal company arrived on the Thursday morning as planned and they were great, they were on time, efficient, and calm. They even joked with us about how much they had to load as they went along, although sadly they had underestimated just how many boxes and items of furniture that we had lined up for them, and we easily filled their lorry, with boxes still left over to be loaded. The plan was agreed that they would return on the Friday morning at 7 a.m. with another small lorry to finish the packing. The fact that Friday was 'the big day' when we had appointments booked at the Notary's office to sell our house and then half an hour later buy our new house didn't faze them at all. No worries they said, we'll just post the spare set of keys back in the letter box when we've finished. We had three sets of keys, so two sets could go to the Notary as required.

So they drove away on the Thursday evening at about 8 p.m. and we breathed a sigh of relief and wandered round our now almost empty shell of a house that had been ours for almost twelve years. It was a strange feeling and it no longer felt like 'home' at all. We were excited about the future and all that promised.

I walked down into our office area, which still looked almost the same as before, as we were leaving all the desks and furniture behind for the new owners. And then my heart stopped for a second.

"Where is the folder I tucked under my desk?" I said to Dave.

"What folder?" came his natural reply.

"Erm, the folder that has ALL of our documents in ready for the sale tomorrow... the most important folder I've been nursing for days," I gasped.

In all the rush and last-minute packing that morning, I had forgotten to put the ubiquitous letter 'X' on the folder. I went cold.

"Oh no, don't tell me it has been packed, please not packed away into that giant lorry of furniture that is currently on its way back to the depot ..." I said, taking in large gulps of air.

Portugal has systems. They like systems, in fact we think that they thrive on them. There is often only one way to do something, you cannot deviate, and as we already knew, the one thing they seem to love more than anything else is paperwork. They really love paperwork, especially hard copies of everything, which are usually in duplicate or even triplicate to be on the safe side.

The missing folder had all the paperwork I thought we would need to complete the sale of our current house – and the purchase of our new house the next morning. I wasn't even sure if the process could happen without the necessary paperwork.

I think I cried at that moment. Weeks and weeks of negotiations, the house-hunting, solicitor hours, and a house now half-empty all around us ... it was just too much to cope with.

Frantically I called the removal company, knowing already what they were going to tell me. The folder wasn't anywhere in the house, we had spent almost an hour searching through every corner and cupboard. It was even worse than I thought, as the driver cheerfully replied,

"Oh yes, I remember packing that little folder under your desk, it was one of the first things I packed, it's right at the front of the lorry."

"Why?" he then innocently asked, "was it important?"

He did kindly offer, at 9 p.m. at night, to try to locate it for me. I told him that was very kind but emptying the entire lorry at that time of night seemed a ridiculous idea, especially as it had taken them almost twelve hours to load it all.

With a heavy heart, and more than a little trepidation, I then called our solicitor at 9.30 p.m. to tell her the news. She was amazingly calm and reassuring, and we talked through everything that we needed legally to be able to complete the sale and purchase the following day. The most important thing she asked was,

"Do you have your passports, or are they in the folder?"

Without passports as legal identification documents we could not proceed. I raced over to my handbag, and there they were. Two passports sat beside my purse. I don't know what made me do it, but I thought they would be safer in my handbag, and I had put them there that morning for safe keeping.

"OK", said the solicitor, "take a deep breath, and we'll check everything else is in order."

I am, by nature, an organiser, which made losing the folder even more of a drama for me. We talked through all the paperwork required, there is a long checklist and we went through every item, and each time the solicitor said,

"That's ok, I've got a copy of that, you sent me that through already, yes I've got that."

I had diligently - almost fanatically - copied her into every single email and document in advance, mostly to check that we had everything in place and that we had not missed anything. Finally we had checked everything, we were back on track, and we were all set for the big day at the Notary office. We had a bottle of champagne chilling in the fridge, but we were so exhausted by the end of the evening that we put a note on it and left it for the new owners to enjoy and crashed to bed.

✿ɠ◌✿ભ✿

Moving Day was as frantic as the day before. We rushed round, let the removal company in, packed the last things in the car, met our friends who were coming with us to babysit Kat for us, and drove over to Portimão to the Notary Office. Helpfully there is a coffee shop next door, which is where we all crashed down and waited for 9.30 a.m. and the office to open.

Huge apologies were of course given to our fabulous solicitor who turned up completely unfazed by the late-night panicked phone call of the previous evening. And then suddenly we were in the Notary's office, everything was being explained and translated for us as we went along, and our buyers were opposite us and seemed as excited as we were.

Cheques were passed across the desk, the bank amusingly sent a man along who picked up the cheque for the outstanding amount of our mortgage, who briefly nodded hello to us, tucked the cheque into his folder, signed a piece of paper and was gone (!) and then we were homeless … for half an hour! Our buyers had been asked to have bankers' drafts made out with precision to cover our subsequent sale, which included two cheques for the owners of the house we were purchasing, and which made the whole process quite painless.

And even though I held my breath every time the Notary asked for a specific piece of paper, all was fine, the deeds were signed, the money handed over, and we were the very excited owners of a house in Aljezur, on the beautiful west coast of the Algarve. We collected Kat, thanked our friends, and we were on our way to our new home and new adventures.

✿ෞ✿ඥ✿

But that is a story that will have to wait until another time ... perhaps I will write a sequel to this book and call it 'Living the Quieter Algarve Dream'.

Postscript: Brexit

I have tried to avoid politics as far as possible throughout this book; however it is inevitable that the subject of Brexit would raise its head.

As we speak, we are now in the Transition Period, before leaving the EU at the end of 2020. The future from the UK perspective is still unknown, but what has been heartening for us living here in Portugal is that the Portuguese government have been both proactive and effusive in their desire to both encourage more people from the UK to consider moving to Portugal; and also active in their desire to reassure current residents that their position here is secure.

The British Ambassador to Portugal has been attending a series of 'surgeries' around the country talking to British overseas residents, and the British Embassy and its staff have been very helpful in informing UK nationals of the requirements for residency, healthcare, driving licences, passports, travel, pets etc. The list is a long one and grows each month.

Last year the Portugal Tourism Board launched its aptly titled 'Brelcome' campaign, playing on a pun between the words 'Brexit' and 'welcome', and the Portuguese government have stated that British people are welcome in Portugal as residents, tourists, investors, and students. They are even considering offering post-Brexit subsidised health care for UK tourists, to ensure that the current European Health Insurance Card (EHIC) healthcare reciprocal scheme can be continued.

We are just happy that we took out our residency all those years ago; and that we now have Permanent Residency status here. We love the country we have chosen to live in; and despite everything that has happened, we still feel welcomed and at home here.

It should not be forgotten that England (now Britain) and Portugal are the world's oldest allies. The history between England and Portugal goes back to 1147 when English crusaders helped King Alfonso I capture Lisbon from the Muslims; and a friendship between the two countries was formed.

In 1386 King Richard II of England agreed the official 'Treaty of Windsor' with King John I of Portugal. English troops had recently helped John drive out a Spanish invasion and it was agreed that they would turn the friendship shown between the two countries into a formal alliance. The key section of the treaty reads: 'If, in time to come, one of the kings or his heir shall need the support of the other, the ally shall be bound to give aid and succour to the other, to the extent required by the danger to his ally's realms, lands, domains, and subjects'.

Let's hope the treaty stands up to the buffering waves of Brexit.

Further Reading

If you are interested in finding out more about moving to live in Portugal, I can recommend the following sites:

The British Embassy in Portugal website
https://www.gov.uk/world/portugal

And the Embassy's Facebook Page: 'Brits in Portugal'
https://www.facebook.com/BritsInPortugal

Also on Facebook – there is a very good and supportive group called 'British Expats in Portugal'. The group has an excellent Files Section with information covering a wide range of 'need to know' hints, tips and guides for anyone considering a move to Portugal.
https://www.facebook.com/groups/265570920476558

Dave Sheldrake Photography. He has a selection of high-quality images of Portugal, and especially his favourite beaches, for you to enjoy. You can view them on his website:
www.davesheldrake.photography/portugal/

If this book has whetted your appetite and you are considering buying in the Algarve, then this article 'Where to Buy a Property in the Algarve' on our Algarve Blog will be a good starting point for you:
https://algarveblog.net/2015/06/10/where-to-buy-a-property-in-the-algarve/

Live and Invest Overseas have a wealth of information and advice for people looking to live or invest abroad. They have in-depth guides, a vast network of correspondents, and free reports and newsletters. They also host regular conferences across the world, including in the Algarve. You can find out more on their website:
https://www.liveandinvestoverseas.com/

Travel Guides:

DK Eyewitness Top 10 Algarve (pocket Travel Guide) (2019)
ISBN: 978-0241355978
This is an easy book to carry around, with informative guides, itineraries and ideas, and handy pull-out maps.

Living in Portugal by Anne de Stoop (2007)
ISBN: 978-2080304858
This is a real treat of a book, with sumptuous photography and detailed descriptions. A book to treasure.

Contacts and Links

Email:
author@alysonsheldrake.com

Our Algarve Blog is full of information, photographs, stories and guides. Feel free to browse and comment:

Algarve Blog website:
https://algarveblog.net/

Algarve Blog on Facebook:
https://www.facebook.com/AlgarveBlog

Alyson's art website:
https://www.alysonsheldrake.com/

Dave's photography website:
https://www.davesheldrake.photography/

Acknowledgements

Thank you to all our friends both here in Portugal and back in the UK. Suz, JP and the Cornets – we still miss you. Jan and Mr Chris, thank you for adding another dimension to our expat life here.

Special thanks to Vicki Good at the Holiday Inn hotel, Armação de Pêra, for offering us our first big break out here.

To all our past, present and future clients – thank you. Your faith in us and our work is much appreciated.

And most of all, thank you to my loving and supportive husband Dave. This one is for you!

Free Photo Book

To view a series of free photographs which accompany this book please visit our Algarve Blog website:

www.algarveblog.net/the-book

Alyson Sheldrake, (2018) *Ferragudo Dream*,
Original Acrylic Painting on Board, Private Collection.

Living the Quieter Algarve
Dream

If you would like to be notified when a sequel to this book is published, please contact the author at

author@alysonsheldrake.com

About the Author

Alyson Sheldrake was born in Birmingham in 1968. She has an Honours Degree in Sport and has a PGCE (Secondary) qualification in Physical Education, English and Drama. She has always loved art and painting, although she found little time for such pleasures, working full-time after graduation. She joined the Devon and Cornwall Police in 1992 and served for thirteen years, before leaving and working her way up the education ladder, rapidly reaching the dizzy heights of Director of Education for the Church of England in Devon in 2008.

Managing over 130 schools in the Devon area was a challenging and demanding role, however after three years her husband Dave retired from the Police, and their long-held dream of living in the sun became a reality.

Alyson handed in her notice, and with her dusty easel and set of acrylic paints packed and ready to move, they started their new adventure living in the beautiful Algarve in Portugal in 2011.

Alyson is the author of the award-winning and popular Algarve Blog, and has also been a keynote speaker for several years at the annual 'Live and Invest in Portugal' international conference.

She is an accomplished and sought-after artist working alongside her husband Dave, a professional photographer. Being able to bring their much-loved hobbies and interests to life has been a wonderful bonus to their new life in the Algarve.

Your Review

I do hope that you have enjoyed reading this book. If you have a moment, I would love it if you could leave a review online, even if it is just a star rating. Though you will not see it, I will do a happy little dance, just like when a painting of mine sells, for every review.

Thank you.

Printed in Great Britain
by Amazon

21761098R00158